Passing the PRINCE2™ Examinations

London: TSO

TSO
information & publishing solutions

Published by TSO (The Stationery Office) and available from:

Online
www.tsoshop.co.uk

Mail, Telephone, Fax & E-mail
TSO
PO Box 29, Norwich, NR3 1GN
Telephone orders/General enquiries:
0870 600 5522
Fax orders: 0870 600 5533
E-mail: customer.services@tso.co.uk
Textphone 0870 240 3701

TSO@Blackwell and other Accredited Agents

Customers can also order publications from:
TSO Ireland
16 Arthur Street, Belfast BT1 4GD
028 9023 8451 Fax 028 9023 5401

First published 2009

ISBN 9780113311903

Printed in the United Kingdom for The Stationery Office
N6215060   c30   08/09

Contents

OGC's foreword

The purpose of this guide is to help people prepare for their PRINCE2™ foundation or practitioner examinations. It will also be useful for those who are coming up to their re-registration examination, as it will serve to jog their memory not only about PRINCE2 but also about the nature of the objective testing exam itself.

The examinations are designed to test your understanding of PRINCE2 from the basic level of knowledge of the method and its vocabulary, through to the ability to apply and modify the method appropriately in a given set of circumstances.

This publication should help pave the way for those preparing to undertake PRINCE2 training, whether through an organized training course, through self-study or by a distance-learning programme. We all have different learning styles, but practice and familiarity with the examination will supplement your understanding of PRINCE2 enabling you to perform at your best.

Thanks go to the APM Group for providing access to the PRINCE2 examination material for the development of this publication.

Finally let me wish you all good luck in preparing for your examinations and in applying PRINCE2 throughout your career.

Jonathan Shebioba
Director of Best Management Practice
Office of Government Commerce

Chief Examiner's foreword

Project management is now recognized and accepted as a profession with a maturity that demands professional standards and training. The PRINCE2 qualification scheme has grown up with the profession and has a history of development and improvement that has led to its adoption by project management professionals world wide.

In 2008, the APM Group moved to an objective test examination approach and in 2009 the revision of PRINCE2 enabled further enhancements to be made to the standards applied to the qualification scheme.

This publication has been developed to support candidates intending to take the foundation and/or practitioner examinations. It includes material that has been developed for the 2009 scheme as well as advice and guidance on how to approach the examinations. The guide reproduces the syllabuses for both examinations, notes for candidates and example papers.

I would recommend that candidates intending to take a PRINCE2 examination review this guidance to familiarize themselves with the different styles of objective test questions used.

Emma Jones
PRINCE2 Chief Examiner

The Official Accreditor's foreword

After extensive consultation involving the user and training communities, 2009 saw the launch of a new edition of *Managing Successful Projects with PRINCE2* (TSO, 2009). There is also a completely new guide for project directors, *Directing Successful Projects with PRINCE2* (TSO, 2009), although this is not included in the qualification scheme.

The essence of this well proven, world-leading project management method is unchanged but there are different emphases on how it is presented. The process structure has been simplified to encourage a flexible approach to applying the method, and greater prominence has been given to the principles that underpin PRINCE2. The guide provides more help for tailoring PRINCE2 to the project environment.

The purpose of this publication is to help candidates prepare for both the foundation and practitioner examinations. It has been developed by Sue Taylor, an experienced PRINCE2 examiner, and reviewed by Emma Jones, the PRINCE2 Chief Examiner, and Graham Williams of GSW Consulting, as part of the APM Group's endorsement process.

As a companion to the material provided by accredited training companies, I believe this guidance will prove invaluable in preparing you for your examinations. I wish you every success, whether you are taking the foundation examination on its own or are progressing to practitioner level.

Richard Pharro
CEO, APM Group

Acknowledgements

AUTHOR

Sue Taylor   APM Group PRINCE2 examiner

The Office of Government Commerce (OGC)
acknowledges with thanks the contribution made
by the APM Group in providing source material
for the syllabus, guidance notes for candidates
and sample papers for use in this publication. OGC
would also like to recognize the contribution of
the following who acted as reviewers of the guide.

REVIEWERS

Emma Jones   PRINCE2 Chief Examiner
Nicola Kelly   APM Group
Graham Williams   GSW Consulting

The PRINCE2 qualifications

1 The PRINCE2 qualifications

1.1 INTRODUCING PRINCE2

PRINCE2 (PRojects IN Controlled Environments) is a project management method which is used extensively in more than 150 countries around the world, and its take-up grows daily. It was originally conceived in the 1970s and since then has grown and developed into the project management method of choice for many international organizations, being widely considered as the world's leading method. It is based on experience drawn from thousands of projects, and from the contributions of countless people involved in projects, including project managers, project teams, academics, trainers, consultants and others. It is generic and can be applied to any project regardless of project scale, type, organization, geography or culture.

PRINCE2 is part of a suite of guidance developed by the UK Office of Government Commerce (OGC), which is aimed at helping organizations and

Figure 1 OGC best-practice guidance

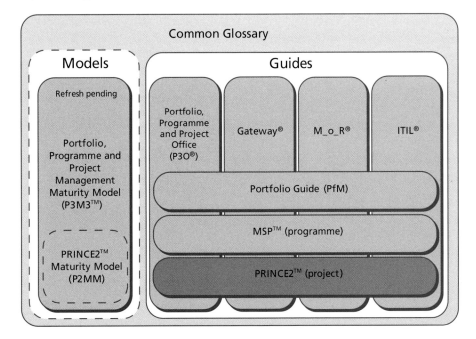

individuals manage their projects, programmes and services consistently and effectively. Figure 1 shows the structure of the set.

Where appropriate, OGC methods and guidance are supported by qualification schemes, and all aspects are supported by accredited training and consultancy services. Please refer to Further Information for more details of other OGC guidance available.

1.2 PRINCE2 QUALIFICATIONS

The examination body for PRINCE2, the APM Group, has offices in Australia, Benelux, China, Denmark, Germany, the United Kingdom and the United States. These offices serve the growing number of candidates who want to take the PRINCE2 examinations, which are available in languages that include Chinese, Danish, Dutch, French, German, Italian, Polish, Portuguese and Spanish. To date, more than 250,000 people hold a PRINCE2 qualification, and examinations have been taken in excess of 100 countries in all continents including Brazil, Latvia, Malaysia, New Zealand, South Africa and the United Arab Emirates, to name but a few. With more than 2,500 examinations being taken every week, the popularity of PRINCE2 continues to grow throughout the world.

There are two levels of PRINCE2 qualification: foundation and practitioner. The foundation level aims to test understanding of the principles and terminology used in PRINCE2. The practitioner level tests the ability of a candidate to apply and tailor PRINCE2 to address the needs and problems of a given project scenario.

1.3 THE PURPOSE OF THIS GUIDE

This guide gives an overview of both the foundation and practitioner qualifications and is designed to help you prepare for the examinations. It has been updated to reflect the changes in the examinations which have arisen from the release of the 2009 edition of the PRINCE2 manual, *Managing Successful Projects with PRINCE2*. It contains:

- Details of the PRINCE2 syllabus, showing the different subject areas of PRINCE2 which could be tested, together with the appropriate learning levels
- An outline of the structure and format of the foundation and practitioner examinations
- A sample paper for each examination, together with rationales for the correct answers
- A description of the different question types which may be included in each examination.

This guide does not attempt to provide you with details of the PRINCE2 method itself. You can find these details in the manual *Managing Successful Projects with PRINCE2*, which is essential reading if you wish to sit the examinations and obtain either level of PRINCE2 qualification.

This guide does not refer to the companion publication *Directing Successful Projects with PRINCE2*, as this is not included in the PRINCE2 syllabus.

The PRINCE2 syllabus

2

2   The PRINCE2 syllabus

Note that the material in this chapter has been taken from the the APM Group document: PRINCE2 2009 – Syllabus V1.1.

2.1   INTRODUCTION

The *Managing Successful Projects with PRINCE2* manual provides guidance on the principles, processes and themes used to manage projects in any environment.

This is a completely revised syllabus based on the new *Managing Successful Projects with PRINCE2* manual issued in June 2009 by OGC and TSO. It reflects the two levels of examination (see Table 1).

The syllabus provides accredited training organizations and candidates with a breakdown of all the learning objectives that are tested in both the PRINCE2 foundation and practitioner examinations. It should therefore form the basis of any learning materials and should be read in conjunction with the PRINCE2 Foundation Exam Candidate Guidance (see section 3.3) and PRINCE2 Practitioner Exam Candidate Guidance (see section 4.4)

2.2   HIGH-LEVEL PERFORMANCE DEFINITION OF A SUCCESSFUL CANDIDATE

The standards expected of registered foundation and practitioner candidates are outlined below.

2.2.1   Foundation

This level aims to measure whether a candidate could act as an informed member of a project management team on a project using the PRINCE2 method, within an environment supporting PRINCE2. To this end, they need to show that they understand the principles and terminology of the method. Specifically they should:

- Understand the purpose and responsibilities of all roles
- Understand the seven principles, the seven themes, the seven processes and the product-based planning and quality review techniques
- Understand which management products are input to, output from and updated in the seven processes
- Understand the purpose of all management products and the composition of the Business Case, Product Descriptions, Issue Report and the Issue, Risk and Quality Registers
- Understand the relationship between the principles, processes, themes, products and roles within a PRINCE2 project.

2.2.2   Practitioner

This level aims to measure whether a candidate could apply PRINCE2 to the running and managing of a non-complex project within an environment supporting PRINCE2. To this end they need to exhibit the competence required for the foundation qualification, and show that they can apply and tailor PRINCE2 to address the needs and problems of a given project scenario. Specifically they should:

Table 1 Comparison between 2005 and 2009 PRINCE2 exams

Examination	Examination format (2005 edition)	Examination format (2009 edition)
Foundation	1 hour	1 hour
	75 questions	75 questions
	Multiple choice	Multiple choice
	50% pass mark	50% pass mark*
	Closed book	Closed book
Practitioner	3 hours	2.5 hours
	Objective test	Objective test
	9 questions	9 questions
	360 possible marks	108 possible marks
	50% pass mark**	55% pass mark
	Open book (PRINCE2 manual only)	Open book (PRINCE2 manual only)
Practitioner re-registration	1 hour	1 hour
	Objective test	Objective test
	3 questions	3 questions
	120 possible marks	36 possible marks
	50% pass mark**	55% pass mark
	Open book (PRINCE2 manual only)	Open book (PRINCE2 manual only)

*The 75 questions within the 2009 edition of the foundation exam will include five trial questions. These five trial questions will not contribute to a candidate's mark. This 50% pass mark is therefore based on a maximum score of 70.

**The pass mark for a practitioner exam based on the 2005 edition is now aligned with the pass mark for the practitioner exam based on the 2009 edition. This took effect on 6 July 2009.

- Know or comment on detailed explanations of all processes, themes and techniques, and worked examples of all PRINCE2 management products as they might be applied to address the particular circumstances of a given project scenario
- Demonstrate that they understand the relationships between processes, themes, techniques and PRINCE2 management products and can apply this understanding
- Demonstrate that they understand the reasons behind the processes, themes and techniques of PRINCE2
- Demonstrate their understanding of how to tailor PRINCE2 to different project environments.

2.3 LEARNING OUTCOMES ASSESSMENT MODEL

2.3.1 Background

A classification widely used when designing assessments for certification and education is Bloom's Taxonomy of Educational Objectives. This classifies learning objectives into six ascending learning levels, each defining a higher degree of competencies and skills. (Bloom *et al.*, 1956, *Taxonomy of Educational Objectives*).

The APM Group has incorporated this into a Learning Outcomes Assessment Model, which is used as a basis for developing the exam qualification scheme and syllabuses.

Use of a six-step learning level in the development of the PRINCE2 exams during 2006/08 demonstrated that a four-step model is more appropriate for this method-based qualification. The model presented here is therefore an adaptation of this generic model specifically for the PRINCE2 qualifications.

2.3.2 Purpose

The purpose of the PRINCE2 Learning Outcomes Assessment Model is to provide a simple and systematic means for assessing and classifying the learning outcomes for the PRINCE2 exams.

The model is used during the syllabus development to help identify the individual learning outcomes and assign each of these to a learning level. These will form the basis of the syllabus topics, with the classification contributing to the assessment of a question's difficulty in the exams. This structured approach helps to ensure that:

- A clear delineation exists in learning level content between different assessments
- Learning outcomes are documented consistently across different areas from the PRINCE2 manual
- Exam questions and papers are created to a consistent level of difficulty.

2.3.3 Levels

Table 2 gives a breakdown of the four levels.

Table 2 The four learning levels used in assessments

1. Knowledge	Able to recall facts from the PRINCE2 manual, including terms, concepts, principles, themes, processes and responsibilities.
2. Comprehension	Understands the principles, processes, themes, the project's environment and roles and can explain how these are applied on/are involved with a project.
3. Application	Demonstrates, for a given scenario, application of the method through: ■ Appropriate use of themes ■ Creation of management products ■ Ability to apply appropriate tailoring of the processes and themes.
4. Evaluation	Ability to evaluate the use of the method through the appraisal of completed products and project events for a given project scenario.

2.4 SYLLABUS PRESENTATION

Each of the subject areas is presented in a similar format as follows:

1. Syllabus area	'Chapter' of the manual
2. Learning outcomes	What you will have to do in order to demonstrate competency in that topic for each level of examination
3. Learning level	Classification of the learning level of each topic against the Learning Outcomes Assessment Model

2.5 SYLLABUS AREAS

Abbreviations for syllabus areas are as follows (reflecting the order in which they appear):

OV	Overview, principles and tailoring PRINCE2 to the project environment
BC	Business Case theme
OR	Organization theme
QU	Quality theme
PL	Plans theme
RK	Risk theme
CH	Change theme
PG	Progress theme
SU	Starting up a Project process
DP	Directing a Project process
IP	Initiating a Project process
CS	Controlling a Stage process
MP	Managing Product Delivery process
SB	Managing a Stage Boundary process
CP	Closing a Project process

Syllabus topic		Syllabus area **Overview, principles and tailoring PRINCE2 to the project environment (OV)**	Foundation	Practitioner	Learning level
Recall facts, terms and concepts relating to the overview, principles and tailoring PRINCE2 to the project environment. Specifically to recall the:					
OV	01	Six aspects of project performance to be managed	✓		1
OV	02	Definition and five characteristics of a project	✓		1
OV	03	Four integrated elements of principles, themes, processes and the project environment upon which PRINCE2 is based	✓		1
OV	04	Benefits of using PRINCE2	✓		1
OV	05	Customer/supplier context of a PRINCE2 project	✓		1
Understand terms and concepts relating to the overview, principles and tailoring PRINCE2 to the project environment, and explain how these are applied on/are involved with a project. Specifically to understand the:					
OV	06	Seven principles	✓		2
OV	07	Difference between a project and a programme	✓		2
OV	08	Characteristics of a project	✓		2
OV	09	Difference between embedding and tailoring PRINCE2		✓	2
OV	10	Context of a customer/supplier environment and how it affects the application of the themes, processes and management products within a project		✓	2
Understand how to tailor the application of PRINCE2 relevant to the size, complexity, risk and importance of a project scenario.					
OV	11	Understand how to tailor the application of PRINCE2 relevant to the size, complexity, risk and importance of a project scenario		✓	3

			Foundation	Practitioner	Learning level
Able to evaluate the tailored application of PRINCE2 in a project scenario.					
OV	12	Able to evaluate the tailored application of PRINCE2 in a project scenario		✓	4

Overview, principles and tailoring PRINCE2 to the project environment will not be treated as a separate question of the objective test practitioner paper, but questions will be included in each of the other syllabus areas.

Syllabus topic		Syllabus area **Business Case (BC) theme**	Foundation	Practitioner	Learning level
Understand how the Business Case theme relates to the principles; the approach to the treatment of this theme; how it is applied throughout the project lifecycle and the responsibilities involved. Specifically to understand:					
BC	01	The purpose of the Business Case theme	✓		2
BC	02	How the Business Case theme supports the continued business justification principle	✓		2
BC	03	The difference between an output, an outcome and a benefit	✓		2
BC	04	The purpose of a Business Case and a Benefits Review Plan	✓		2
BC	05	The recommended composition of a Business Case	✓		2
BC	06	In which process(es) the Business Case is developed, verified, maintained and confirmed and which roles are responsible for this		✓	2
BC	07	The relationship between a programme's business case and a project's Business Case		✓	2
BC	08	The recommended composition of a Benefits Review Plan, in which process(es) it is developed and reviewed and which roles are responsible for this		✓	2

continues

Business Case (BC) theme continued

Understand how to apply and tailor the relevant aspects of the Business Case theme to a project scenario, when creating products or making decisions related to this theme, in any or all of the processes. Specifically to:					
BC	09	Apply the Business Case theme appropriately to a project scenario when creating or updating, using the recommended composition, the following products: ■ Business Case ■ Benefits Review Plan		✓	3
BC	10	Identify outputs, outcomes and benefits for a project scenario		✓	3
Able to evaluate the appropriateness of the application of the Business Case theme throughout the lifecycle of a project scenario. Specifically to evaluate:					
BC	11	Use of the Business Case theme when creating or updating the following products, using the recommended composition, for a project scenario: ■ Business Case ■ Benefits Review Plan		✓	4

The different types of Business Case and the various techniques that can be used for Investment Appraisal will not be tested within the foundation or practitioner qualification.

Syllabus topic		Syllabus area **Organization (OR) theme**	Foundation	Practitioner	Learning level
OR	01	Recall the defined roles within the Organization theme.	✓		1
Understand how the Organization theme relates to the principles; the approach to the treatment of this theme; how it is applied throughout the project lifecycle and the responsibilities involved. Specifically to understand:					
OR	02	The purpose of the Organization theme	✓		2

OR	03	How the Organization theme supports the defined roles and responsibilities principle	✓		2
OR	04	In which process(es) the Organization theme is applied and which roles are responsible for this	✓		2
OR	05	The three project interests and how these are represented within the three levels of the project management team structure	✓		2
OR	06	How the four levels of the project management structure apply to the process model	✓		2
OR	07	The role of the: ■ Project Board ■ Project Manager ■ Project Assurance ■ Change Authority ■ Team Manager ■ Project Support and how each is used throughout the processes and other themes	✓		2
OR	08	The difference between project stakeholders and project decision makers	✓		2
OR	09	The purpose of the Communication Management Strategy	✓		2
OR	10	The relationship between the Communication Management Strategy and other products and themes		✓	2
OR	11	The recommended composition of a Communication Management Strategy, in which process(es) it is developed and reviewed and which roles are responsible for this		✓	2

continues

Organization (OR) theme continued

Understand how to apply and tailor the relevant aspects of the Organization theme to a project scenario, when creating products or making decisions related to this theme, in any or all of the processes. Specifically to:					
OR	12	Apply the Organization theme appropriately to a project scenario when creating or updating, using the recommended composition, the following products: ■ Project management team structure, including acceptable role consolidations or sharing ■ Communication Management Strategy ■ Role descriptions		✓	3
Able to evaluate the appropriateness of the application of the Organization theme throughout the lifecycle of a project scenario. Specifically to evaluate:					
OR	13	Use of the following products, using the recommended composition, for a project scenario: ■ Project management team structure ■ Communication Management Strategy ■ Role descriptions		✓	4

Stakeholder engagement will not be tested within the foundation or practitioner qualifications.

Syllabus topic		Syllabus area **Quality (QU) theme**	Foundation	Practitioner	Learning level
QU	01	Recall the recommended quality review team roles and their responsibilities	✓		1
Understand how the Quality theme relates to the principles; the approach to the treatment of this theme; how it is applied throughout the project lifecycle and the responsibilities involved. Specifically to understand:					
QU	02	The purpose of the Quality theme	✓		2

QU	03	How the Quality theme supports the 'learn from experience' principle	✓		2
QU	04	The relationship between quality assurance and Project Assurance	✓		2
QU	05	The objectives of the quality review technique	✓		2
QU	06	The purpose of: ■ Quality planning ■ Customer's quality expectations ■ Quality Register ■ Quality Management Strategy ■ Quality control	✓		2
QU	07	The purpose and composition of a Product Description	✓		2
QU	08	The PRINCE2 approach to quality – quality audit trail		✓	2
QU	09	How the customer's quality expectations are derived, in which process(es) and which roles are responsible for this		✓	2
QU	10	How quality interfaces with quality management systems		✓	2
QU	11	In which process(es) Product Descriptions are developed and reviewed and which roles are responsible for this		✓	2
QU	12	The recommended composition of a Quality Management Strategy, in which process(es) it is developed and reviewed and which roles are responsible for this		✓	2
Understand how to apply and tailor the relevant aspects of the Quality theme to a project scenario, when creating products or making decisions related to this theme, in any or all of the processes. **Specifically to:**					
QU	13	Apply the Quality theme appropriately to a project scenario when creating or updating, using the recommended composition, the following products: ■ Project Product Description ■ Quality headings (excluding quality method) of a Product Description for a given product ■ Quality Register ■ Quality Management Strategy		✓	3

continues

Quality (QU) theme continued

QU	14	Apply the quality review technique to a given product within a project scenario		✓	3
Able to evaluate the appropriateness of the application of the Quality theme throughout the lifecycle of a project scenario. Specifically to evaluate:					
QU	15	Use of the following products, using the recommended composition, for a project scenario: ■ Project Product Description ■ Quality headings (excluding quality method) of a Product Description ■ Quality Register ■ Quality Management Strategy		✓	4
QU	16	Use of the quality review technique for a given product within a project scenario		✓	4

Quality methods, side-benefits of the quality review technique and the purpose of quality inspection will not be tested within the foundation or practitioner qualifications.

Syllabus topic		Syllabus area **Plans (PL) theme**	Foundation	Practitioner	Learning level
Recall facts, terms and concepts relating to the Plans theme. Specifically to recall the:					
PL	01	Levels of plan recommended by PRINCE2	✓		1
PL	02	Steps in producing a PRINCE2 plan	✓		1
PL	03	Four tasks of product-based planning	✓		1
Understand how the Plans theme relates to the principles; the approach to the treatment of this theme; how it is applied throughout the project lifecycle and the responsibilities involved. Specifically to understand:					

PL	04	The purpose of the Plans theme	✓		2
PL	05	The levels of plans, their purpose and the interrelationship between the Project Plan, Stage Plans, Team Plans and an Exception Plan	✓		2
PL	06	The three types of management product: baselines, records and reports	✓		2
PL	07	The product-based planning technique	✓		2
PL	08	How the Plans theme supports the principles of: ■ Focus on products ■ Manage by exception ■ Manage by stages	✓		2
PL	09	The recommended composition of a plan, in which process(es) it is developed, reviewed and updated, and which roles are responsible for this		✓	2
Understand how to apply and tailor the relevant aspects of the Plans theme to a project scenario, when creating products or making decisions related to this theme, in any or all of the processes. **Specifically to:**					
PL	10	Apply the Plans theme appropriately to a project scenario when creating or updating, using the recommended composition, a plan (excluding the schedule)		✓	3
PL	11	Apply the product-based planning technique to a given project scenario		✓	3
Able to evaluate the appropriateness of the application of the Plans theme throughout the lifecycle of a project scenario. **Specifically to evaluate:**					
PL	12	Use of a plan (excluding the schedule), using the recommended composition, for a project scenario		✓	4
PL	13	Product-based planning technique applied to a project scenario		✓	4

Techniques and planning rules used for estimating or scheduling will not be tested within the foundation or practitioner qualifications.

Syllabus topic		Syllabus area **Risk (RK) theme**	Foundation	Practitioner	Learning level
	Recall facts, terms and concepts relating to the Risk theme. Specifically to recall:			
RK	01	The definition of a risk and the difference between a threat and an opportunity	✓		1
RK	02	The risk response types and whether they are used to respond to a threat or an opportunity	✓		1
RK	03	The difference between a risk owner and a risk actionee	✓		1
	Understand how the Risk theme relates to the principles; the approach to the treatment of this theme; how it is applied throughout the project lifecycle and the responsibilities involved. Specifically to understand:			
RK	04	The purpose of the Risk theme	✓		2
RK	05	How the Risk theme supports the continued business justification principle	✓		2
RK	06	The five steps within the risk management procedure	✓		2
RK	07	The purpose of a risk budget	✓		2
RK	08	The probability, impact and proximity of a risk	✓		2
RK	09	The difference between cause, event and effect when expressing a risk	✓		2
RK	10	The concept of risk appetite/tolerances	✓		2
RK	11	The purpose of a: ■ Risk Management Strategy ■ Risk Register	✓		2
RK	12	The recommended composition of a Risk Management Strategy; in which process(es) it is developed, reviewed and updated; and which roles are responsible for this		✓	2

RK	13	The concept of inherent, secondary and residual risks		✓	2
Understand how to apply and tailor the relevant aspects of the Risk theme to a project scenario, when creating products or making decisions related to this theme, in any or all of the processes. **Specifically to:**					
RK	14	Apply the Risk theme appropriately to a project scenario when creating or updating, using the recommended composition, the following products: ▪ Risk Management Strategy ▪ Risk Register		✓	3
RK	15	Apply the five steps (identify, assess, plan, implement and communicate) within the risk management procedure to a project scenario		✓	3
RK	16	Identify risks for a project scenario		✓	3
RK	17	Identify primary and secondary risks and estimate inherent and residual risks for a project scenario		✓	3
Able to evaluate the appropriateness of the application of the Risk theme throughout the lifecycle of a project scenario. **Specifically to evaluate:**					
RK	18	Use of the following products, using the recommended composition, for a project scenario: ▪ Risk Management Strategy ▪ Risk Register		✓	4
RK	19	Application of risk management to a project scenario		✓	4

Levels of risk management, risk identification techniques, risk estimation techniques and risk evaluation techniques will not be tested within the foundation or practitioner qualifications.

Syllabus topic		Syllabus area **Change (CH) theme**	Foundation	Practitioner	Learning level
Recall facts, terms and concepts relating to the Change theme. Specifically to recall the:					
CH	01	Three types of issue	✓		1
Understand how the Change theme relates to the principles; the approach to the treatment of this theme; how it is applied throughout the project lifecycle and the responsibilities involved. Specifically to understand:					
CH	02	The purpose of the Change theme	✓		2
CH	03	The purpose of a change budget and Change Authority	✓		2
CH	04	The purpose and recommended composition of an: ▪ Issue Report ▪ Issue Register	✓		2
CH	05	The purpose of a: ▪ Configuration Management Strategy ▪ Configuration Item Record ▪ Product Status Account	✓		2
CH	06	How the Change theme supports the manage by exception principle	✓		2
CH	07	The issue and change control procedure	✓		2
CH	08	In which process(es) issues are captured and managed, and which roles are responsible		✓	2
CH	09	In which process(es) an Issue Register is developed, reviewed and updated, and which roles are responsible		✓	2
CH	10	In which process(es) a change budget and a Change Authority are agreed and which roles are responsible		✓	2

CH	11	The recommended composition of a: ■ Configuration Management Strategy ■ Configuration Item Record ■ Product Status Account and in which process(es) they are created, reviewed and updated, and which roles are responsible		✓	2
Understand how to apply and tailor the relevant aspects of the Change theme to a project scenario, when creating products or making decisions related to this theme, in any or all of the processes. Specifically to:					
CH	12	Apply the Change theme appropriately to a project scenario when creating or updating, using the recommended composition, the following products: ■ Issue Report ■ Issue Register ■ Configuration Management Strategy ■ Configuration Item Record for a given product ■ Product Status Account		✓	3
CH	13	Identify the appropriate type for a given issue		✓	3
CH	14	Apply the issue and change control procedure to a project scenario		✓	3
CH	15	Identify appropriate resource(s) for the role of Change Authority within a project scenario		✓	3

continues

Change (CH) theme continued

		Able to evaluate the appropriateness of the application of the Change theme throughout the lifecycle of a project scenario. Specifically to evaluate:			
CH	16	Use of the following products, using the recommended composition, for a project scenario: ■ Issue Report ■ Issue Register ■ Configuration Management Strategy ■ Configuration Item Record for a given product ■ Product Status Account		✓	4
CH	17	Application of the issue and change control procedure to a project scenario		✓	4

Syllabus topic		Syllabus area **Progress (PG) theme**	Foundation	Practitioner	Learning level
Recall facts, terms and concepts relating to the Progress theme. Specifically to recall the:					
PG	01	Event-driven and time-driven controls	✓		1
PG	02	Reporting channels between the levels of management	✓		1
Understand how the Progress theme relates to the principles; the approach to the treatment of this theme; how it is applied throughout the project lifecycle and the responsibilities involved. Specifically to understand:					
PG	03	The purpose of the Progress theme	✓		2
PG	04	The concept of management stages	✓		2

PG	05	How the Progress theme supports the principles of: ▪ Manage by stages ▪ Learn from experience ▪ Manage by exception	✓		2
PG	06	The difference between management and technical stages	✓		2
PG	07	The factors to consider in identifying management stages	✓		2
PG	08	Tolerance(s): where they may be usefully applied; in which management products they are documented and how management by exception applies to the different levels of management	✓		2
PG	09	The purpose of a: ▪ Daily Log ▪ Work Package ▪ Lessons Log ▪ Checkpoint Report ▪ Highlight Report ▪ End Stage Report ▪ Exception Report ▪ End Project Report ▪ Issue Report ▪ Lessons Report	✓		2
PG	10	The recommended composition of a: ▪ Work Package ▪ Lessons Log ▪ Checkpoint Report ▪ Highlight Report ▪ End Stage Report ▪ Exception Report ▪ End Project Report ▪ Lessons Report and in which process(es) they are created and approved, and which roles are responsible		✓	2

continues

Progress (PG) theme continued

		Understand how to apply and tailor the relevant aspects of the Progress theme to a project scenario, when creating products or making decisions related to this theme, in any or all of the processes. Specifically to:			
PG	11	Apply the Progress theme appropriately to a project scenario when creating or updating, using the recommended composition, the following products: ■ Work Package ■ Lessons Log ■ Checkpoint Report ■ Highlight Report ■ End Stage Report ■ Exception Report ■ End Project Report ■ Issue Report ■ Lessons Report		✓	3
PG	12	Apply the concept of management by exception to a project scenario		✓	3
		Able to evaluate the appropriateness of the application of the Progress theme throughout the lifecycle of a project scenario. Specifically to evaluate:			
PG	13	Use of the following products, using the recommended composition, for a project scenario: ■ Work Package ■ Lessons Log ■ Checkpoint Report ■ Highlight Report ■ End Stage Report ■ Exception Report ■ End Project Report ■ Issue Report ■ Lessons Report		✓	4
PG	14	Application of management by exception to a project scenario		✓	4

Progress evaluation techniques will not be tested within the foundation or practitioner qualifications.

Syllabus topic		Syllabus area **Starting up a Project (SU) process**	Foundation	Practitioner	Learning level
SU	01	Recall the stated purpose and triggers of the SU process	✓		1
Understand the SU process and how it can be applied and tailored on a project. Specifically to understand:					
SU	02	The objectives and context of the SU process	✓		2
SU	03	How the SU process supports the seven PRINCE2 principles	✓		2
SU	04	The activities within the SU process	✓		2
SU	05	The responsibilities within the activities of the SU process	✓		2
SU	06	The purpose of a: ■ Project Brief ■ Project Product Description	✓		2
SU	07	How the seven themes can be applied within the SU process		✓	2
SU	08	The recommended composition of the following: ■ Lessons Log ■ Project Brief ■ Project Product Description ■ Outline Business Case ■ Stage Plan ■ Project management team role descriptions		✓	2

continues

Starting up a Project (SU) process continued

Understand how to apply the SU process, tailoring the recommended activities and actions where appropriate, to a project scenario. Specifically to:					
SU	09	Apply the recommended SU process actions to a project scenario to create or update, using the recommended composition, the following products: ■ Lessons Log ■ Project Brief ■ Outline Business Case ■ Stage Plan ■ Project Product Description ■ Project management team role descriptions		✓	3
SU	10	Apply the recommended SU process actions to a project scenario		✓	3
Able to evaluate the application of the SU process to a project scenario, by assessing whether the relevant activities of the process were correctly applied. Specifically to evaluate:					
SU	11	Using the recommended composition, the use of the following products in the SU process for a project scenario: ■ Lessons Log ■ Project Brief ■ Outline Business Case ■ Stage Plan ■ Project Product Description ■ Project management team role descriptions		✓	4
SU	12	The application of the recommended SU process actions for a project scenario		✓	4

Syllabus topic		Syllabus area **Directing a Project (DP) process**	Foundation	Practitioner	Learning level
DP	01	Recall the stated purpose and triggers of the DP process	✓		1
Understand the DP process and how it can be applied and tailored on a project. Specifically to understand:					
DP	02	The objectives and context of the DP process	✓		2
DP	03	How the DP process supports the seven PRINCE2 principles	✓		2
DP	04	The activities within the DP process	✓		2
DP	05	The responsibilities within the activities of the DP process	✓		2
DP	06	The use of the inputs to and outputs from the DP process	✓		2
DP	07	How the seven themes can be applied within the DP process		✓	2
Able to evaluate the application of the recommended DP process actions for a project scenario.					
DP	08	Able to evaluate the application of the recommended DP process actions for a project scenario		✓	4

Syllabus topic		Syllabus area **Initiating a Project (IP) process**	Foundation	Practitioner	Learning level
IP	01	Recall the stated purpose and triggers of the IP process	✓		1
Understand the IP process and how it can be applied and tailored to a project. Specifically to understand:					
IP	02	The objectives and context of the IP process	✓		2
IP	03	How the IP process supports the seven PRINCE2 principles	✓		2
IP	04	The activities within the IP process	✓		2
IP	05	The responsibilities within the activities of the IP process	✓		2
IP	06	The use of the following inputs in the IP process: ■ Daily Log ■ Lessons Log ■ Project Brief ■ Project Product Description ■ Outline Business Case	✓		2
IP	07	The purpose of a Project Initiation Documentation (PID)	✓		2
IP	08	The recommended composition of a: ■ Business Case ■ Product Description ■ Risk Register ■ Issue Register ■ Quality Register	✓		2

IP	09	How the seven themes can be applied within the IP 9rocess		✓	2

IP	10	The recommended composition of a:
		
		  ▪ Communication Management Strategy
		  ▪ Quality Management Strategy
		  ▪ Configuration Management Strategy
		  ▪ Risk Management Strategy
		  ▪ Project Plan
		  ▪ PID
		  ▪ Configuration Item Record
		  ▪ Benefits Review Plan
				✓	2

Understand how to apply the IP process, tailoring the recommended activities and actions where appropriate, to a project scenario. **Specifically to:**					

IP	11	Apply the recommended IP process actions to a project scenario to create or update, using the recommended composition, the following products:
		
		  ▪ Communication Management Strategy
		  ▪ Quality Management Strategy
		  ▪ Configuration Management Strategy
		  ▪ Risk Management Strategy
		  ▪ Project Plan
		  ▪ Business Case
		  ▪ Risk Register
		  ▪ Issue Register
		  ▪ Quality Register
		  ▪ Configuration Item Record
		  ▪ Benefits Review Plan
				✓	3

IP	12	Apply the recommended IP process actions to a project scenario		✓	3

continues

Initiating a Project (IP) process continued

Able to evaluate the application of the IP process to a project scenario, by assessing whether the relevant activities of the process were correctly applied. Specifically to evaluate:					
IP	13	Using the recommended composition, the use of the following products in the IP Process for a project scenario: ■ Communication Management Strategy ■ Quality Management Strategy ■ Configuration Management Strategy ■ Risk Management Strategy ■ Project Plan ■ Business Case ■ PID ■ Risk Register ■ Issue Register ■ Quality Register ■ Configuration Item Record ■ Benefits Review Plan		✓	4
IP	14	The application of the recommended IP process actions for a project scenario		✓	4

Syllabus topic		Syllabus area **Controlling a Stage (CS) process**	Foundation	Practitioner	Learning level
CS	01	Recall the stated purpose and triggers of the CS process	✓		1
Understand the CS process and how it can be applied and tailored on a project. Specifically to understand:					
CS	02	The objectives and context of the CS process	✓		2
CS	03	How the CS process supports the seven PRINCE2 principles	✓		2

CS	04	The activities within the CS process	✓		2
CS	05	The responsibilities within the activities of the CS process	✓		2
CS	06	The use of the following inputs in the CS process: ▪ PID ▪ Issue Report ▪ Issue Register ▪ Risk Register ▪ Quality Register ▪ Checkpoint Report ▪ Plans ▪ Product Description ▪ Configuration Item Record ▪ Product Status Account ▪ Lessons Log	✓		2
CS	07	The recommended composition of an Issue Report	✓		2
CS	08	How the seven themes can be applied within the CS process		✓	2
CS	09	The recommended composition of a: ▪ Work Package ▪ Highlight Report		✓	2

continues

Controlling a Stage (CS) process continued

Understand how to apply the CS process, tailoring the recommended activities and actions where appropriate, to a project scenario. Specifically to:					
CS	10	Apply the recommended CS process actions to a project scenario to create or update, using the recommended composition, the following products: ■ Work Package ■ Highlight Report ■ Exception Report ■ Issue Report ■ Issue Register ■ Risk Register ■ Quality Register ■ Stage Plan ■ Configuration Item Record ■ Product Status Account ■ Lessons Log		✓	3
CS	11	Apply the recommended CS process actions to a project scenario		✓	3
Able to evaluate the application of the CS process to a project scenario, by assessing whether the relevant activities of the process were correctly applied. Specifically to evaluate:					
CS	12	Using the recommended composition, the use of the following products in the CS process for a project scenario: ■ Work Package ■ Highlight Report ■ Exception Report ■ Issue Report ■ Issue Register ■ Risk Register ■ Quality Register ■ Stage Plan ■ Configuration Item Record ■ Product Status Account ■ Lessons Log		✓	4

| CS | 13 | The application of the recommended CS process actions for a given project scenario | | ✓ | 4 |

Syllabus topic		Syllabus area **Managing Product Delivery (MP) process**	Foundation	Practitioner	Learning level
MP	01	Recall the stated purpose and triggers of the MP process	✓		1
Understand the MP process and how it can be applied and tailored on a project. Specifically to understand:					
MP	02	The objectives and context of the MP process	✓		2
MP	03	How the MP process supports the seven PRINCE2 principles	✓		2
MP	04	The activities within the MP process	✓		2
MP	05	The responsibilities within the activities of the MP process	✓		2
MP	06	The use of the following inputs in the MP process: ■ Work Package ■ Product Description	✓		2
MP	07	How the seven themes can be applied within the MP process		✓	2
MP	08	The recommended composition of a Checkpoint Report		✓	2
Understand how to apply the MP process, tailoring the recommended activities and actions where appropriate, to a project scenario. Specifically to:					

continues

Managing Product Delivery (MP) process continued

				Foundation	Practitioner	Learning level
MP	09	Apply the recommended MP process actions to a project scenario to create or update, using the recommended composition, the following products: ■ Work Package ■ Checkpoint Report ■ Product Description ■ Quality Register ■ Issue Report ■ Configuration Item Record			✓	3
MP	10	Apply the recommended MP process actions to a project scenario			✓	3
Able to evaluate the application of the MP process to a project scenario by assessing whether the relevant activities of the process were correctly applied. Specifically to evaluate:						
MP	11	Using the recommended composition, the use of the following products in the MP process for a project scenario: ■ Work Package ■ Checkpoint Report ■ Product Description ■ Quality Register ■ Issue Report ■ Configuration Item Record			✓	4
MP	12	The application of the recommended MP process actions for a given project scenario			✓	4

Syllabus topic		Syllabus area **Managing a Stage Boundary (SB) process**	Foundation	Practitioner	Learning level
SB	01	Recall the stated purpose and triggers of the SB process	✓		1
Understand the SB process and how it can be applied and tailored on a project. Specifically to understand:					

SB	02	The objectives and context of the SB process	✓		2
SB	03	How the SB process supports the seven PRINCE2 principles	✓		2
SB	04	The activities within the SB process	✓		2
SB	05	The responsibilities within the activities of the SB process	✓		2
SB	06	▪ The use of the following inputs in the SB process: ▪ PID ▪ Project Plan ▪ Business Case ▪ Quality Management Strategy ▪ Risk Management Strategy ▪ Communication Management Strategy ▪ Configuration Management Strategy ▪ Stage Plan ▪ Exception Report ▪ Configuration Item Record ▪ Product Status Account ▪ Benefits Review Plan ▪ Issue Register ▪ Quality Register ▪ Risk Register ▪ Lessons Log	✓		2
SB	07	How the seven themes can be applied within the SB process		✓	2
SB	08	The recommended composition of a: ▪ Stage Plan ▪ Configuration Item Record ▪ End Stage Report ▪ Exception Plan ▪ Product Status Account ▪ Lessons Report		✓	2

continues

Managing a Stage Boundary (SB) process continued

Understand how to apply the SB process, tailoring the recommended activities and actions where appropriate, to a project scenario. Specifically to:					
SB	09	Apply the recommended SB process actions to a project scenario to create or update, using the recommended composition, the following products: ■ Stage Plan ■ Project Plan ■ End Stage Report ■ Exception Plan ■ Product Status Account ■ Business Case ■ Benefits Review Plan ■ Issue Register ■ Quality Register ■ Risk Register ■ Product Description ■ Configuration Item Record ■ PID ■ Lessons Report ■ Project management team structure		✓	3
SB	10	Apply the recommended SB process actions to a project scenario		✓	3

			Foundation	Practitioner	Learning level
Able to evaluate the application of the SB process to a project scenario, by assessing whether the relevant activities of the process were correctly applied. Specifically to evaluate:					
SB	11	Using the recommended composition, the use of the following products in the SB process for a project scenario: ▪ Stage Plan ▪ Project Plan ▪ End Stage Report ▪ Exception Plan ▪ Product Status Account ▪ Business Case ▪ Benefits Review Plan ▪ Issue Register ▪ Quality Register ▪ Risk Register ▪ Product Description ▪ Configuration Item Record ▪ PID ▪ Lessons Report ▪ Project management team structure		✓	4
SB	12	The application of the recommended SB process actions to a project scenario		✓	4

Syllabus topic		Syllabus area **Closing a Project (CP) process**	Foundation	Practitioner	Learning level
CP	01	Recall the stated purpose and triggers of the CP process	✓		1
Understand the CP process and how it can be applied and tailored on a project. Specifically to understand:					

continues

Closing a Project (CP) process continued

CP	02	The objectives and context of the CP process	✓		2
CP	03	How the CP process supports the seven PRINCE2 principles	✓		2
CP	04	The activities within the CP process	✓		2
CP	05	The responsibilities within the activities of the CP process	✓		2
CP	06	The use of the following inputs in the CP process: ■ Product Status Account ■ PID ■ Benefits Review Plan ■ Project Product Description ■ Lessons Log ■ Project Plan ■ Issue Register ■ Risk Register ■ Quality Register ■ Risk Management Strategy ■ Configuration Management Strategy ■ Communication Management Strategy ■ Quality Management Strategy	✓		2
CP	07	How the seven themes can be applied within the CP process		✓	2
CP	08	The recommended composition of a: ■ End Project Report ■ Lessons Report ■ Benefits Review Plan		✓	2

		Understand how to apply the CP process, tailoring the recommended activities and actions where appropriate, to a project scenario. Specifically to:			
CP	09	Apply the recommended CP process actions to a project scenario to create or update, using the recommended composition, the following products: ■ End Project Report ■ Lessons Report ■ Benefits Review Plan		✓	3
CP	10	Apply the recommended CP process actions to a project scenario		✓	3
		Able to evaluate the application of the CP process to a project scenario, by assessing whether the relevant activities of the process were correctly applied. Specifically to evaluate:			
CP	11	Using the recommended composition, the use of the following products in the CP process for a project scenario: ■ Issue Register ■ Risk Register ■ Quality Register ■ Daily Log ■ End Project Report ■ Lessons Report ■ Benefits Review Plan		✓	4
CP	12	The application of the recommended CP process actions to a project scenario		✓	4

The foundation examination

3

3   The foundation examination

3.1   STRUCTURE OF THE EXAMINATION

The foundation examination is a one-hour, closed-book examination. It is designed to test knowledge of PRINCE2 by providing a selection of possible answers from which candidates must choose the correct one. There are 75 questions in all, but five of these are trial questions which are not scored. The total possible score for the foundation is therefore 70. The pass mark is 50% or more of the marks, i.e. 35 or more marks out of 70. All questions gain one mark for a correct answer, and there is no negative marking.

In normal circumstances, papers will be marked immediately after the examination has taken place and candidates will be informed of their results by the invigilator who marked their paper. At open-centre examinations there may not be time to mark the paper immediately afterwards, and so candidates will be emailed their results within five working days of the examination.

3.2   HINTS AND TIPS

The best technique for the foundation examination is to go through the paper in a first non-stop 'sweep', answering all the straightforward questions to which you know the answers; ignore any long questions or those which will take longer to work out. When you have completed the first sweep you should have most of the questions answered.

Now return to the more difficult questions in a second sweep. Many will not be as tricky as they first appeared and, with a bit of common sense

and careful reading of the question, you should be able to discount many of the options presented. This may leave you with one option which, on re-examination, is clearly the correct one. For other questions, you may be left with, say, two options from which you still cannot choose. Leave these and continue the second sweep. You should now feel confident that you are well beyond the pass mark and still have time to spare.

Return for a third sweep through those few outstanding questions. Review the question and the remaining options. For some, the answer may now suggest itself. For the others, think about them again, but before time runs out, at least make a guess. You should have at least a fifty-fifty chance of being right.

Beware of changing answers you have already made – general experience indicates that there are probably as many changes made from correct to incorrect answers as there are from incorrect to correct! If you do need to make a change, however, make sure you show it clearly.

3.3   APM GROUP CANDIDATE GUIDANCE – FOUNDATION

The next section contains the candidate guidance, issued by the APM Group, which gives details of the foundation examination and the question types used. The guidance has been taken from the APM Group's document: PRINCE2 – Foundation Exam – Candidate Guidance V1.2. When you have read this you should be ready to try the foundation examination paper included later in this chapter.

PRINCE2 FOUNDATION EXAM CANDIDATE GUIDANCE

1 Introduction

1.1 The objective of the examination is to enable a candidate to demonstrate an understanding of the PRINCE2 principles, processes, themes, techniques and roles. The foundation exam uses objective test questions which require a candidate to choose a response to a question from a set of choices, only one of which is correct.

1.2 The following paragraphs explain the format of the question papers and the different styles of question asked. There are also some suggestions on how to approach answering the various styles of question.

2 Structure of the paper

The examination paper consists of:

2.1 A Question Booklet which contains 75 questions – 70 exam questions and five trial questions – each covering a different syllabus topic. Each of the 70 questions is worth one mark, but the trial questions are not scored. The use of trial questions enables new questions to be trialled without affecting candidates' marks. The pass mark is 35. You are expected to answer all questions. There will be no indication of which questions are exam questions and which are trial.

2.2 The Answer Sheet in which your answers must be given. There will only ever be one answer to each question. If more than one answer is given in the Answer Sheet the response line will be void and will attract no marks. Marks are not subtracted for incorrect answers.

3 PRINCE2 syllabus areas addressed

The exam consists of 75 questions in total, which cover all 15 areas of the PRINCE2 foundation syllabus. The full PRINCE2 syllabus is available from the APM Group or from your accredited training organization.

4 Styles of question

There are a number of different test styles used within the paper. All test styles are based on the selection of the correct answer from a choice of four options.

The test styles are:

4.1 Standard

Which individual role is ultimately accountable for the project?

    a   Executive
    b   Project Manager
    c   Senior Supplier
    d   Senior User

4.2 Negative

Which is NOT one of the key elements to balance when defining management stages?

    a   The availability of the Project Board
    b   How far ahead in the project it is sensible to plan
    c   The amount of risk within a project
    d   How confident the Project Board and Project Manager are in proceeding

4.3 Missing word

Identify the missing words in the following sentence.

The reasons for undertaking the project must drive the [?] and should be used to continually align the project progress to the business objectives.

    a   delivery strategy
    b   decision making
    c   benefits management strategy
    d   tolerance approach

4.4 List

When reviewing the status of a Work Package, what does the Project Manager look at?

1. Checkpoint Reports
2. Business Case
3. Quality Register
4. Team Plans
    a   1, 2, 3
    b   1, 2, 4
    c   1, 3, 4
    d   2, 3, 4

5 Time management

The exam is 60 minutes in duration. Candidates must manage their time in order to complete all questions. All 75 questions should be attempted. If candidates wish to write their answers on the question paper first, they must be aware of the additional time needed to complete the Answer Sheet. Only answers submitted on the Answer Sheet provided will contribute to the result.

No support material is permitted. This is a closed-book exam.

6 Using the Answer Sheet

The Answer Sheet will be read electronically and the results generated by computer. It is therefore essential that candidates follow the instructions given and mark their answers accordingly. Failure to do so may lead to delay and, in some cases, answers being void.

All answers are given by the candidate filling in 'ovals' that relate to their chosen response, as shown in the figure below.

Example of format used in Answer Sheet

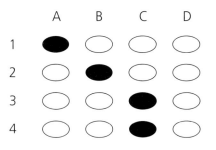

The oval must be filled in **in pencil, not pen**. If a pen is used, the answers will not be marked.

Acceptable ways to complete the Answer Sheet are either by completely filling in the oval, or drawing a horizontal line through the centre of the oval. Any other method, including ticks or crosses, is not acceptable and will not be marked.

If a candidate wishes to change their answer during the exam, the incorrect answer should be erased completely and the correct answer indicated. If more than one answer is given by the candidate, the question will score zero, as only one answer is required.

3.4 SAMPLE FOUNDATION PAPER

Note that the material in this section has been taken from the APM Group's document: PRINCE2 2009 Foundation Exam – Sample Paper 1 – V1.0.

PRINCE2™

The Foundation Examination

SAMPLE PAPER 1 V1.0

MULTIPLE CHOICE

1 HOUR PAPER

INSTRUCTIONS

1. All 75 questions should be attempted.
2. There are no trick questions.
3. All answers are to be marked on the answer grid provided.
4. Please use a pencil and NOT ink to mark your answers in the Answer Sheet provided. There is only one correct answer per question.
5. You have 1 hour for this paper.
6. You must get 35 or more correct to pass.

Candidate Number: ....………...

1 Which is one of the six aspects of a project performance that we wish to manage?

   a   Performance
   b   Reliability
   c   Scope
   d   Ease of use

2 How does the Controlling a Stage process support the learn from experience principle?

   a   Supports the Project Manager in ensuring products are delivered within the tolerances agreed with the Project Board
   b   Encourages the Project Manager to review the progress of the stage and log any lessons
   c   Requires escalation of issues and risks to the Project Board which threatens the stage or project tolerances
   d   Recommends a Work Package is created to deliver products that require specific skills

3 Which process is triggered by the request to initiate a project?

   a   Starting up a Project
   b   Initiating a Project
   c   Directing a Project
   d   Managing a Stage Boundary

4 The purpose of which theme is to establish mechanisms to monitor and compare actual achievements against those planned?

   a   Business Case
   b   Change
   c   Progress
   d   Quality

5 What is an objective of the Closing a Project process?

   a   Checks that all the project's products have been signed off by the users
   b   Prepares for the final stage of the project
   c   Captures the customer's quality expectations
   d   Ensures that all benefits have been achieved

6 Identify the missing words in the following sentence.

A purpose of the Managing a Stage Boundary process is to provide the Project Board with sufficient information so that it can approve the [?] for the next stage.

   a   Work Packages
   b   Exception Report
   c   Stage Plan
   d   Project Brief

7 Which theme provides information on what is required, how it will be achieved and by whom?

   a   Organization
   b   Plans
   c   Business Case
   d   Quality

8 Which role is responsible for capturing the customer's quality expectations?

   a   Project Manager
   b   Executive
   c   Senior Supplier
   d   Senior User

9 Basing projects on a 'management by exception' framework provides which benefit?

    a Promotes consistency of project work
    b Project is not seen as an end in itself
    c Clarity of what a project will deliver, why, when and by whom
    d Efficient and economic use of management time

10 Which are purposes of the Initiating a Project process?

    1. Establishes a firm base for the project
    2. Ensures there is a clear understanding of the work involved to deliver the project's products
    3. Avoids commitment of funds before it is appropriate to do so
    4. Makes sufficient information available to define and prepare the Project Brief
        a 1, 2, 3
        b 1, 2, 4
        c 1, 3, 4
        d 2, 3, 4

11 What is the purpose of the Managing Product Delivery process?

    a Controls the link between the Project Manager and the Team Manager(s)
    b Tracks the progress of a stage through the consolidation of Checkpoint Reports
    c Provides a link between the work of the Project Manager and the Project Board
    d Maintains a focus on the delivery of benefits throughout the stage

12 Which role is responsible for authorizing and monitoring work to be completed and for taking corrective action within a stage?

    a Project Manager
    b Project Support
    c Project Assurance
    d Team Manager

13 Which fact is true of Project Assurance but not quality assurance?

    a Responsible for monitoring the conduct of the project
    b Independent of the Project Manager
    c Appointed as part of the project management team
    d Responsible for reviewing the project for compliance with corporate standards

14 Which statement does NOT define a characteristic of a project?

    a Has a higher degree of risk than business as usual
    b Involves people with different skills introducing a change that will impact others outside of the team
    c Has a lifespan that usually covers the delivery of the desired outcomes and the realization of the expected benefits
    d A temporary management structure created for the implementation of business products

15 Which product forms the 'contract' between the Project Manager and the Project Board for the project?

    a Project Plan
    b Project Product Description
    c Project Initiation Documentation
    d Project Brief

16 What is an objective of the Managing a Stage Boundary process?

    a   Enables the Project Board to commit resources and expenditure required for the initiation stage

    b   Reviews and, if necessary, updates the Project Initiation Documentation

    c   Provides a controlled break between those managing the project and those creating products

    d   Ensures a periodic review is held to approve the products created within the completed stage

17 Which of the following is a baseline management product?

    a   Benefits Review Plan

    b   Issue Register

    c   Highlight Report

    d   Product Status Account

18 What is a stated purpose of the Closing a Project process?

    a   Define the procedure for handing over products

    b   Provide a fixed point at which acceptance for the project product is confirmed

    c   Capture the lessons identified during the last stage

    d   Confirm all project benefits have been achieved

19 What does a Product Description contain?

    1.   A breakdown of the individual parts that make up the product

    2.   The management stage in which the product is to be created

    3.   Details of the individuals responsible for reviewing the product

    4.   Any allowable deviation from the specified quality criteria

    a   1, 2, 3

    b   1, 2, 4

    c   1, 3, 4

    d   2, 3, 4

20 What is a Product Description used for in the Controlling a Stage process?

    a   Demonstrating that a product meets its quality criteria by applying the method specified

    b   Forming part of a Work Package

    c   Developing the product(s) to the defined quality criteria

    d   Obtaining approval for completed products from the authorities identified therein

21 What is a purpose of a Checkpoint Report?

    a   Provides progress information on all of the Work Packages within a stage

    b   Updates the Project Manager on the status of a Work Package

    c   Records results of all quality checks and quality reviews held during the stage

    d   Provides details of Work Packages to be issued before the next report is due

22 Which of the PRINCE2 principles supports the definition of tolerances for the six project objectives?

   a   Manage by stages
   b   Tailor to suit the project environment
   c   Focus on products
   d   Manage by exception

23 When would the Project Board first confirm the customer's quality expectations?

   a   Authorizing initiation
   b   Authorizing the project
   c   Giving ad hoc direction
   d   Authorizing a Stage or Exception Plan

24 Which is one of the four integrated elements within PRINCE2?

   a   Quality
   b   Role descriptions
   c   Processes
   d   Product Descriptions

25 How does the Starting up a Project process support the manage by stages principle?

   a   Provides a structured set of activities for the pre-project stage of the PRINCE2 journey
   b   Determines the level of authority delegated to the Project Manager for the initiation stage
   c   Ensures time is not wasted initiating a project based on unsound assumptions
   d   Ensures that the work required for project initiation is planned

26 How does the Managing a Stage Boundary process support the focus on products principle?

   a   Prepares and distributes an interim report on what has gone well
   b   Documents the agreed level of quality for each of the deliverables of the next stage
   c   Replans a stage in response to a forecast deviation from tolerance
   d   Reviews and if necessary updates the project management team for the next stage

27 What is a benefit of adopting the product-based planning technique?

   a   All the required products of the project will be delivered to time and to cost
   b   Clearly shows how long a project will take and highlights those products on the critical path
   c   It removes the need for activity-based planning
   d   Reduces the risk of incorrectly scoping the project

28 Which is a reason for reviewing the Project Brief during the Initiating a Project process?

   a   Provides details of the selected solution to be delivered by the project
   b   Describes lessons to be learned from similar projects
   c   Identifies risks and issues associated with configuration management
   d   Confirms the time and cost tolerances for the next stage

29 Which project management team role can trigger a premature closure of a project?

a   Project Manager
b   Project Board
c   Corporate or programme management
d   Project Assurance

30 Which is a purpose of the Organization theme?

a   Establish tolerances around the resources utilized on the project
b   Provide project management training to those working within the project
c   Establish a strategy for communication between all interested parties of the project
d   Implement the controls required to permit management by exception

31 Which of the following takes place before the initiation of a project?

1.   Provide the Executive with a role description
2.   Consider the successes and failures of similar activities carried out in the past
3.   Record and update all initial risks in the Daily Log
4.   Develop the detailed Business Case stating why the project is worth doing
   a   1, 2, 3
   b   1, 2, 4
   c   1, 3, 4
   d   2, 3, 4

32 Which is the first plan to be created?

a   Project Plan
b   Stage Plan
c   Team Plan
d   Exception Plan

33 Which process interfaces with corporate or programme management to provide and receive information?

a   Managing Product Delivery
b   Directing a Project
c   Controlling a Stage
d   Managing a Stage Boundary

34 What does the Managing Product Delivery process NOT aim to ensure?

a   Suppliers understand what is expected of them
b   Products of appropriate quality are delivered
c   The Project Board is kept informed of progress on the products
d   Work for the team is agreed with the Project Manager

35 Which is an objective of the quality review technique?

a   Involve key interested parties in promoting wider acceptance
b   Develop and improve the specification of a product through continuous assessment
c   Correct any typographical errors found in a product and obtain sign-off during the quality review meeting
d   Update the status information in the Configuration Item Record when a product is signed-off

36 How is the Risk Register used in the Managing a Stage Boundary process?

    a   Checked for any Issue Reports noted for review at stage end

    b   Reviewed for the status of risks

    c   Updated to record that all risks have been closed

    d   Checked to ensure that all open risks have been transferred to the Issue Register

37 Identify the missing words in the following sentence.

Any requests for change, which require Project Board approval, should be recorded in the [?] and their status monitored by the Project Manager

    a   Product Description

    b   Issue Register

    c   Configuration Item Record

    d   Quality Register

38 What is a purpose of the Project Brief?

    a   Defines the project, to form the basis for its management and the assessment of overall success

    b   Outlines any lessons from previous projects and how they may affect this project

    c   Communicates the quality techniques and standards to be applied to achieve the required quality levels

    d   Provides a firm basis on which to initiate the project

39 If a product fails its quality check, which product should always be updated?

    a   Risk Register

    b   Issue Register

    c   Quality Register

    d   Lessons Log

40 How does the Business Case theme support the continued business justification principle?

    a   Allows projects not delivering direct benefits to proceed without a Business Case

    b   Removes the need for a separate Business Case where a project is part of a programme

    c   Mandates that even the simplest of projects should have a Business Case

    d   Ensures a new Business Case is created at the end of each stage to confirm the viability of the next stage

41 How does the Managing Product Delivery process support the manage by exception principle?

    a   By breaking work down into stages that are easier to plan

    b   Using Team Managers who have experience in the work

    c   Team Managers should warn the Project Manager of any threat to the tolerances that are defined in the Work Package

    d   Team Managers create an Exception Report for events beyond Work Package limits

42 Which is a purpose of the Starting up a Project process?

    a   Ensuring that the prerequisites for initiating the project are in place

    b   Establishing that the Project Plan can meet the required target dates

    c   Creating the Project Initiation Documentation so the project can be initiated

    d   Confirming to corporate or programme management that quality expectations will be met

43 Which is recommended as a possible risk response type for an opportunity?

    a   Reduce

    b   Transfer

    c   Reject

    d   Fallback

44 Which action is NOT taken by the Project Board?

    a   Allocate tolerance to specialist teams

    b   Transfer ownership of the Benefits Review Plan to corporate or programme management

    c   Approve the Project Product Description

    d   Confirm the required frequency of Highlight Reports

45 Who sets the project tolerances?

    a   Project Board

    b   Corporate/programme management

    c   Executive

    d   Project Manager

46 After the first stage, when are the Stage Plans for further stages produced?

    a   Near the end of the current stage

    b   After completion of the current stage

    c   When creating the Project Plan

    d   At the start of the initiation stage

47 What levels of plan are recommended by PRINCE2?

    a   Project Plan

    b   Project Plan and Stage Plan

    c   Project Plan, Stage Plan and Team Plan

    d   Project Plan, Stage Plan, Team Plan and Exception Plan

48 Identify the missing words in the following sentence.

The Team Plan should be checked by [?] to ensure that it is technically feasible.

    a   User Assurance

    b   Supplier Assurance

    c   Business Assurance

    d   Quality Assurance

49 How does the Initiating a Project process support the continued business justification principle?

    a   Confirms who is to be involved in the project decision-making

    b   Clarifies the products to be delivered

    c   Documents how the corporate project management method will be tailored to suit the project

    d   Refines the Business Case

50 What is risk appetite?

   a   Part of the project budget, used to pay for any additional activities required to manage risks

   b   The funds the Project Board is willing to spend on the management of risk

   c   Permissible deviation from planned expenditure without the need to escalate to the next higher authority

   d   An organization's attitude towards risk exposure

51 Who represents the 'delivering' level on the project management team?

   a   Project Board

   b   Project Manager

   c   Team Manager

   d   Project Support

52 What is a purpose of the Benefits Review Plan?

   a   Documents the justification for the undertaking of a project

   b   Describes only residual benefits and those that could not be achieved during the lifecycle of the project

   c   Provides a schedule of activities to measure achievement of those benefits which could not be measured during the project

   d   Provides the timescales over which the benefits will be realized, for entry into the Business Case

53 What is a purpose of a Configuration Item Record?

   a   Provides a summary of the status of all products at any one time

   b   Provides any details of important links between project products

   c   Supports the creation of the product breakdown structure

   d   Includes an analysis of any Issue Report or risk which caused the product to change

54 Which is NOT a purpose of the Controlling a Stage process?

   a   Take corrective actions to control deviations from the Stage Plan

   b   Recommend the time and cost tolerance for the stage

   c   Report progress to the Project Board

   d   Assign work to be done

55 Which statement is true of stages?

   a   A project can be scheduled without management stages

   b   There can be several management stages within a technical stage

   c   Several management stages can be scheduled to run concurrently

   d   Technical stages and management stages should always end together

56 What is a purpose of the Risk Management Strategy?

   a Defines the techniques to be used when assessing project threats and opportunities

   b Summarizes exposure to strategic, programme, project and operational threats and opportunities

   c Recommends responses for each of the project threats and opportunities

   d Identifies suitable risk owners for each of the project threats and opportunities

57 Identify the missing words in the following sentence.

   If the Project Manager needs to know the results of a quality review, reviewing the [?] will provide a summary together with the date of any follow-up meeting.

   a Stage Plan

   b Issue Register

   c Daily Log

   d Quality Register

58 What are the three recommended types of issue?

   a Off-specification, request for change and concession

   b Off-specification, request for change and problem or concern

   c Request for change, problem or concern, and Issue Report

   d Request for change, Issue Report and risk

59 What is established within the Initiating a Project process?

   a How the project is going to be approached

   b How the required quality will be achieved

   c All the information to develop the Project Brief is available

   d Any constraints that could affect the project have been removed

60 Which term is used to identify when a risk might materialize?

   a Impact

   b Proximity

   c Probability

   d Evaluate

61 How does the Progress theme support the manage by exception principle?

   a Provides for technical stages which can overlap

   b Ensures decision points are scheduled throughout the project to assess the viability of the project

   c Recommends actions which may improve the outcome of future projects

   d Provides for delegation of a unit of work within a defined level of authority

62 Identify the missing words in the following sentence.

   If a Project Manager has the appropriate specialist skills and knowledge, there may be no need to appoint [?] to the project.

   a Senior Supplier(s)

   b Team Manager(s)

   c Project Assurance

   d Senior User(s)

63 Which statement is true for project stakeholders?

  a Some have decision-making authority within the project environment

  b All are all external to the corporate organization

  c All are internal to the project management team structure

  d None have decision-making authority within the project environment

64 What is a risk budget used to fund?

  a Potential changes that may be required as the project progresses

  b Shortfall in estimating the development costs of the project's products

  c Additional activities to reduce, avoid, fallback, transfer, share or enhance project risks

  d Assessment of project risks and the planning of any responses to deal with these

65 Which are objectives of the Controlling a Stage process?

  1. Watch for, and assess, any issues and risks that arise

  2. Escalate threats to budgets, timescales or benefits

  3. Focus attention on delivery of the stage's products

  4. Produce the Stage Plan for the next stage

      a 1, 2, 3

      b 1, 2, 4

      c 1, 3, 4

      d 2, 3, 4

66 Which of the following represents an output?

  a New accounting procedures

  b Staffing costs reduced by 20%

  c Faster and more accurate processing of all sales invoices

  d Quick access to all detailed reports and accounts

67 What is a purpose of the Quality theme?

  a Ensure that all products of the project meet business expectations

  b Address the procedures and responsibilities for the creation, maintenance and control of project products

  c Clearly define the method of delivering the project's products

  d Enable the assessment of continuing project viability

68 What should influence the length of a management stage?

  a An exception situation forecast to happen due to unexpected costs

  b The level of project risk

  c Availability of the Project Board

  d Requirement of a specialist team for an element of the development work

69 How is the Configuration Management Strategy used in the Closing a Project process?

   1. Reviewed for its effectiveness in controlling and protecting all products

   2. Examined to confirm how all project files are to be archived

   3. Referenced to establish how all products need to be handed over into the relevant operational environment(s)

   4. Updated to incorporate any corporate or programme policies and processes that applied to the project

     a 1, 2, 3
     b 1, 2, 4
     c 1, 3, 4
     d 2, 3, 4

70 What is a risk cause?

   a Negative consequence of a threat occurring

   b Explanation of the event(s) which, should they occur, would create a problem

   c Positive consequence of an opportunity exploited

   d A known situation which creates uncertainty

71 Which product is a time-driven control?

   a End Stage Report
   b Exception Report
   c Checkpoint Report
   d Lessons Report

72 When does PRINCE2 say the project management team should be considered for updating?

   a As and when new stakeholders are identified

   b When planning a quality review, the producer, reviewer(s), chair and administrator will need to be added

   c At the end of each stage, when preparing the Stage Plan for the next stage

   d During product creation, if a member of the delivery team is not available and has to be replaced

73 What is a purpose of the Change Authority?

   a Determines the change budget for a project

   b Assesses the impact of all requests for change

   c Reduces the number of requests for change that need to be escalated to the Project Board

   d Allows the Project Board to delegate the approval of all risks and Issue Reports

74 What would you NOT find in a Business Case?

   a Major potential threats to the expected costs and benefits

   b Details of the existing situation, how this needs to change and why

   c A forecast of what will happen if the project is not approved

   d The names of those people responsible for achieving the benefits

75 What is the first step within the
recommended risk management procedure?

a Identify
b Assess
c Plan
d Implement

PRINCE2 foundation examination
Answer key

Week ending:

For Exam Paper: GB – PRINCE2 2009 Foundation Exam – Sample Paper 1 V1.0

Question	Answer	Syllabus topic	Section
1	C	OV01	1.5.2
2	B	CS03	15.4.4/2.1
3	C	DP01	13.4.1
4	C	PG03	10.1
5	A	CP02	18.2
6	C	SB01	17.1
7	B	PL04	7.1
8	A	SU05	12.4.4
9	D	OV04	1.7
10	A	IP01	14.1
11	A	MP01	16.1
12	A	CS05	15.1
13	C	QU04	6.2.6
14	C	OV08	1.3
15	C	IP07	A.20
16	B	SB02	17.2
17	A	PL06	Appendix A
18	B	CP01	18.1

Note that the material in this section has been taken from the APM Group's document: GB – PRINCE2 2009 Foundation Exam – Sample Paper 1 – V1.0 Answer Key.

Question	Answer	Syllabus topic	Section
19	C	QU07	A.17.2
20	B	CS06.8	15.4.1
21	B	PG09.4	10.3.3.4
22	D	OV06	2.5
23	A	DP04	13.4.1
24	C	OV03	1.5.3
25	D	SU03	12.2
26	B	SB03	2
27	D	PL07	7.3.3
28	A	IP06.3	14.4.6
29	B	CP05	18.4.2
30	C	OR02	5.1
31	A	SU04	14.4.7
32	B	PL05	11.2.1
33	B	DP02	13.2
34	C	MP02	16.2
35	A	QU05	6.3.2.1
36	B	SB06.15	17.4.1
37	B	CH04.2	A.12.1
38	D	SU06.1	A.19.1
39	C	IP08.5	6.3.1.6
40	C	BC02	4.1
41	C	MP03	16.4.2/2.5
42	A	SU01	12.1
43	C	RK02	Table 8.2
44	A	DP05	15.4.1

Question	Answer	Syllabus topic	Section
45	B	PG08	10.3.1.1
46	A	SB04	17.4.1
47	C	PL01	7.2.3
48	B	MP05	16.4.1
49	D	IP03	2.1/14.2
50	D	RK10	8.3.2
51	C	OR06	5.3.1
52	C	BC04	A1.1
53	B	CH05.2	A.5.1
54	B	CS01	15.1
55	B	PG06	10.3.2.3
56	A	RK11.1	A.24.1
57	D	QU06.3	A.23.1
58	B	CH01	Table 9.1
59	B	IP04	14.4.3
60	B	RK08	8.3.5.2
61	D	PG05.3	2.5
62	B	OR07.5	5.3.2.7
63	A	OR08	5.2.5
64	C	RK07	8.3.6
65	A	CS02	15.2
66	A	BC03	4.2.2
67	A	QU02	6.1
68	B	PG07	10.3.2.2
69	A	CP06.11	18.4
70	D	RK09	8.3.5.1

Question	Answer	Syllabus topic	Section
71	C	PG01	10.3.3
72	C	OR04	17.4.1
73	C	CH03	9.3.1.1
74	D	BC05	A2.2
75	A	RK06	8.3.5

The practitioner examination

4

4 The practitioner examination

4.1 STRUCTURE OF THE EXAMINATION

The practitioner examination is a 2.5-hour examination consisting of nine questions, all of which have to be answered. Each question is made up of two to four part-questions, each of which will contain a number of question items. Each question item is worth one mark, with each question totalling 12 marks. No negative marks are awarded. The pass mark is 55%.

The PRINCE2 manual *Managing Successful Projects with PRINCE2* is the only reference material allowed into the examination room.

As the aim of the examination is to test the ability of a candidate to apply the PRINCE2 method in practice, the examination is based around a scenario which describes an organization and a project to be managed using PRINCE2. The questions test the use of the method by applying the PRINCE2 themes and processes to the scenario. Each question will test one of the seven themes or a process area.

The practitioner paper combines the following process syllabus areas:

- Starting Up a Project and Initiating a Project
- Managing a Stage Boundary, Closing a Project and Directing a Project
- Controlling a Stage and Managing Product Delivery

Process questions will cover one or more processes from these process areas.

The overall focus of the paper is on the themes, because these provide guidance on how actions within the processes will be undertaken. **Theme** questions test understanding of the theme across the project lifecycle, or look at a more in-depth examination of product aspects relating to that theme. **Process** questions test understanding of how to apply or evaluate the actions from a process, including how to tailor the process.

The examination paper consists of three booklets.

- The **Scenario Booklet** contains one scenario which describes the business organization and gives details of the project. The Scenario Booklet also contains additional information if this is needed to answer specific questions.
- The **Question Booklet** contains the nine questions, each covering a different syllabus area. Each question:
  - is worth a total of 12 marks, with a total of 108 marks for the paper
  - is made up of two to four part-questions, each of which is itself made up of a number of question items. Each question item is worth a single mark
- The **Answer Booklet** contains the answer sheets on which you must mark your answers. There will only ever be one correct answer to each question, unless the question clearly states otherwise.

4.2 QUESTION TYPES

The practitioner paper uses a number of different multiple-choice question types. These include:

- **Classic** – 'choose **one** from a list' of possible answers. The correct response is to be selected from a list of three or four options.
- **Multiple response** – 'choose **two** correct options from a list'. This question follows exactly the same format as the 'classic' test type, but two answers are required from a list of five options. It is **the only question style that requires more than one response to gain a mark**. If more or fewer than two responses are given then the answer will be void.
- **Matching** – involves linking items in one list to items in a second list. There is **only one correct response** to each question item.
- **Sequence matching** – events to be positioned in a sequence. The activities in column 1 have to be placed in the sequence in which they should be performed. The candidate selects an option from column 2 for each activity in column 1.
- **Assertion/reason** – each item consists of two statements, an assertion and a reason that are linked by the word 'because'. The candidate must determine whether the statements are true and, if so, whether the reason explains why the assertion is true.

The candidate guidance issued by the APM Group, included later in this chapter, contains further details of the examination and examples of each question type.

4.3 HINTS AND TIPS

As all the questions in the practitioner examination must be answered, many people go through the paper in order from start to finish. However, all the questions in the practitioner paper are stand-alone and, therefore, you can answer them in any order. If you are stronger in certain syllabus areas, it might give you a feeling of confidence if you answer those questions first.

Whatever your preferred approach, the key is to ensure you are familiar with the syllabus topics and the different question types. Use the candidate guidance and the sample paper to help with this. Look at the rationale for each question and make sure you understand the logic between the correct and incorrect answers. If you are unsure, refer back to the manual reference included in the rationale.

Some questions require you to analyse the project scenario or the additional information provided in order to answer the question. Where this is required, it will be clearly stated in the question text. Other questions contain a number of statements which are all true for the project, but which are not expressed correctly in PRINCE2 terms. You do not need to refer to the project scenario or additional information to answer these but to use your knowledge of PRINCE2 to decide which option is expressed correctly in the context of PRINCE2.

You are allowed to take the manual *Managing Successful Projects with PRINCE2* into the examination room for reference. You might find it useful to mark this up using tabs to separate the themes, processes and Product Descriptions so that you can easily refer to each one of these during the examination.

You should also be aware of some of the terms which are used in specific ways in the questions, as this will affect the type of analysis which is required. For example:

- '**Should**' is used to test whether something should be done in a scenario situation because it is consistent with PRINCE2's principles and recommended practices. For example, take the scenario statement 'The label design competition should be planned and managed as two management stages.' In order to establish whether this statement is true or false you will have to evaluate whether or not it is consistent with the recommendations PRINCE2 makes when determining management stages.
- '**Must**' is used when something is mandatory.
- '**Will**' and '**is**' are used to describe indisputable facts about PRINCE2, e.g. 'In PRINCE2, the Business Case is developed at the beginning of the project.'

Refer to the candidate guidance for further discussion on the use of these and other terms.

4.4 APM GROUP CANDIDATE GUIDANCE – PRACTITIONER

Note that the material in this section has been taken from the APM Group's document: PRINCE2 2009 – Practitioner Exam – Candidate Guidance V1.2.

PRINCE2 PRACTITIONER EXAM CANDIDATE GUIDANCE

1 Introduction

1.1 The objectives of the examination are to enable a candidate to demonstrate an understanding of PRINCE2 and an ability to apply the method in an appropriate way in a given set of circumstances described in a scenario. The practitioner exam uses objective test questions which require a candidate to select a response to a question from a set of choices, only one of which is correct.

1.2 The following paragraphs explain the format of the question papers, and the different types of question asked. There are also some suggestions on how to approach answering the various types of question.

1.3 The PRINCE2 Registered Practitioner qualification is valid for five years. Practitioners should be re-registered within 3–5 years of their original certification in order to demonstrate their commitment to professional development. Details of the practitioner re-registration examination can be found at section 9.

2 Structure of the paper

The examination paper consists of three booklets.

2.1 The **Scenario Booklet** will contain one scenario providing a description of the organization, the business rationale for the project and the project objectives. The Scenario Booklet may also provide additional information for one or more of the nine questions. Where additional information is to be used, this is clearly stated in bold within the question. **Additional information is only to be used for the question to which it relates**.

If there is no reference to additional information or the project scenario within a question, then answer the question using only the information contained within the question. **In this case the project scenario provides the background and context to the overall project but not the facts required to answer the question**.

2.2 The **Question Booklet** will contain nine questions, each covering a different syllabus area which will be clearly identified at the beginning of each question. Each of the nine questions contains 12 question lines, each of which attracts one mark, giving a total of 108 marks. The pass mark is 59 (55%). Each of the nine questions will be sub-divided into parts. Each of the 'part-questions' will identify the portion of the 12 marks allocated to it. You are expected to answer all questions and part-questions.

2.3 The **Answer Booklet** will contain the answer sheets on which your answers must be given. There will only ever be one answer to each question unless it is clearly stated otherwise within the question. If more than one answer is given in the Answer Booklet, but not required by the question, the response line will be void.

3 PRINCE2 syllabus areas addressed

The PRINCE2 syllabus contains 15 defined syllabus areas covering each of the seven themes, each of the seven processes and an overview area also covering the principles and tailoring PRINCE2 to a project environment.

Within the practitioner examination, there will be seven 'theme' questions, each testing one of the seven themes, and two 'process group' questions, which will test two of the three groups of processes as identified below. Each **question** will test a minimum of two syllabus topics from within the syllabus area.

Syllabus area
Business Case theme
Organization theme
Quality theme
Plans theme
Risk theme
Change theme
Progress theme
Starting up a Project and Initiating a Project processes
Directing a Project, Managing a Stage Boundary and Closing a Project processes
Controlling a Stage and Managing Product Delivery processes

The overview, principles and tailoring PRINCE2 to the project environment syllabus area will not be examined separately, but details from this syllabus section may be included in the questions on each of the other syllabus areas. The full PRINCE2 syllabus is available from the APM Group or from your accredited training organization.

4 Types of question

There are five different types of question used within the paper.

4.1 **Classic multiple-choice questions** – 'choose **one** from a list of possible options'. The correct response is to be selected from a list of three or four options.

Answer the following question about the relationship between the Communication Management Strategy and other PRINCE2 products and themes.	
Which statement correctly describes the relationship between the Communication Management Strategy and the Organization theme?	
A	The Communication Management Strategy is approved by the Project Manager.
B	The Communication Management Strategy includes the information flow, both to the interested stakeholders from the project and from the interested stakeholders to the project.
C	All identified stakeholders should review the Communication Management Strategy.

4.2   Multiple response – 'choose two correct options from a list of five options'. This question follows exactly the same format as the 'classic style', but more than one answer is required. It is **the only question type that requires more than one response to gain a mark**. Both responses must be correct to gain a mark. If more or fewer than two responses are given then the answer will be void.

Answer the following question about the use of the **configuration management procedure** section of the Configuration Management Strategy.		
Remember to limit your answers to the number of selections requested in the question.		
1	**Verification and audit**: Which **2** areas would be reviewed when doing a configuration audit?	
	A	The entries in the Project Product Description are correctly specified.
	B	Specialist products are identified correctly.
	C	A product matches the state recorded in its Configuration Item Record.
	D	The retrieval of products is following the configuration management procedure.
	E	Risks to products are being assessed according to the Risk Management Strategy.

4.3 **Matching** – 'link items in one list to items in a second list'. There is **only one correct response** to each question, but options from the second list may be used once, more than once or not at all.

	Column 1	Column 2
	Column 1 is a list of **true statements** from the Starting up a Project process. For each statement in Column 1, select from Column 2 the product in which the statement should have been recorded. Each selection from Column 2 can be used once, more than once or not at all.	
1	The feasibility study must be approved by the Board of Directors before any development on the new project can commence.	A Lessons Log
2	The company could ignore the recommendation from the feasibility study and NOT produce the new product.	B Outline Business Case C Stage Plan D Project Product Description E Project management team role descriptions
3	Other new product developments have suffered adversely when the business areas were not involved during the development of the products.	
4	70% of the people from the trial group must confirm that they would buy the new product.	

4.4   Sequencing – 'position events in a sequence'.
The example below demonstrates a sequencing
question based on the matching type question.

Column 1 is a list of decisions to be made within the project. For each decision in Column 1, decide whether or not it is made in the Starting up a Project process and indicate in which order the decisions which are made should occur.		
	Column 1	Column 2
1	Approval of the feasibility study by the Project Board before any work on the project can commence.	A NOT made in the Starting up a Project process
2	Decide if the source of funding is sufficient to fund the project's objective.	B First
3	Assess which parties should be involved during the project, as suggested by previous development projects.	C Second
		D Third
4	Evaluate two possible candidates for Project Manager and decide which should be appointed.	E Fourth

4.5   Assertion/reason – 'evaluate two
statements (an assertion and a reason) to
determine if either, both or neither is true and, if
both are true, whether the reason explains why the
assertion is true'. If either statement is false, the
answer is selected from options C, D or E. If both
statements are true, a third step is required. If the
reason explains why the assertion is true, the
answer is A. If it does not, the answer is B.

Using the project scenario, answer the following question.

Lines 1 to 2 in the table below consist of an assertion statement and a reason statement. For each line identify the appropriate option, from options A to E, that applies. Each option can be used once, more than once or not at all.

Option	Assertion	Reason	
A	True	True	AND the reason explains the assertion
B	True	True	BUT the reason does not explain the assertion
C	True	False	
D	False	True	
E	False	False	

	Assertion		Reason
1	The expected benefits from increasing staff flexibility should be included in the Business Case.		All known Business Case benefits should be described clearly in measurable terms.
2	The expected benefits from increasing staff flexibility should be included in the Business Case.		Information about expected project benefits forms part of the justification for undertaking a project.

For example, in question 1 and 2 of the example provided above, the assertion statement is true but the answer to question 1 is a B and question 2 an A.

In question 1 the reason statement is true; however, the fact that benefits should be described in measurable terms does not explain why the benefit of increased staff flexibility should be documented in the Business Case. The answer is B.

In question 2 the reason statement provides an explanation for the assertion. From the scenario information it will be clear that staff flexibility is a projected benefit for this project and from PRINCE2 we know that the Business Case provides justification for undertaking the project, based on the estimated costs against the anticipated benefits to be gained. The reason is true and explains the assertion. The answer is therefore A.

There is **only one correct response** to each question, but options can be used once, more than once or not at all.

5 Learning levels

Part-questions will vary in their level of difficulty depending on the learning objective of the test. The learning levels are:

1 Knowledge
2 Comprehension
3 Application
4 Evaluation.

The four learning levels used in assessments

1. Knowledge	Able to recall facts from the PRINCE2 manual, including terms, concepts, principles, themes, processes and responsibilities.
2. Comprehension	Understands the principles, processes, themes, the project's environment and roles and can explain how these are applied on/are involved with a project.
3. Application	Demonstrates application of the method through: ■ appropriate use of themes ■ creation of management products ■ ability to apply appropriate tailoring of the processes and themes for a given scenario.
4. Evaluation	Ability to evaluate the use of the method through the appraisal of completed products and project events for a given project scenario.

Within a question, the part-questions will be assembled in order of ascending learning level.

The focus of the exam is on the application and evaluation learning objectives. A whole paper will contain a maximum of 10 marks in total for level two questions and no level one questions.

6 Time management

The exam is 150 minutes in duration. Candidates must manage their time in order to complete all questions. As a general guide, candidates may wish to spend the first five minutes reading the scenario information and getting familiar with the layout of the paper. If 15 minutes is then allocated for each of the nine questions, this will allow 10 minutes' tolerance for additional reading required for some questions. This suggested timing is for guidance only.

Reference to the candidate's own annotated PRINCE2 manual is permitted during the exam. **No additional support material** is permitted; this includes Post-it notes (other than tabulation of the sections of the manual) and stapled sheets.

Candidates should be aware of the time constraint upon them. Whilst the manual is there for support, as in real life, the time pressure of the exam means that the questions **have not been designed** on the basis that candidates are required or even expected to use the manual to answer questions. Its use is optional. As a guide, a candidate might check the manual once or twice in an exam for a specific point, but any more than that is likely to be counter-productive and is not advised.

7 Editorial notes

7.1 Throughout the Scenario Booklet and Question Booklet, title case has been used for all references to PRINCE2 themes, processes, defined management products and proper nouns.

7.2 Uses of 'should', 'will' and 'must'
'Should' is used to express obligation – something that is good or important or recommended. It is less strong than must and is used to test whether something should be done in a scenario situation because it is consistent with the principles and recommended practices of PRINCE2.

Consider the following statement, 'The Finance Director should perform the Executive role on the project.'

Given the scenario information provided, the Finance Director may or may not be the appropriate candidate for the PRINCE2 Executive role, in terms of ability to perform the PRINCE2 responsibilities for that role and represent the business interest on the project. Use of 'should' requires the reader to evaluate this.

'Must' is used when talking about something that is 'necessary' or 'has' to occur, i.e. something that is mandatory.

'Will' and 'is', however, are used to express something definite, or indisputable facts about PRINCE2; e.g. to describe generic facts about the PRINCE2 products, processes, themes and techniques such as 'The acceptance criteria are documented in the Project Product Description'.

7.3 Use of 'appropriate'

In the context of the practitioner exam, the use of 'appropriate' in the example below means 'is the statement an appropriate entry in terms of the recommended composition of the Business Case, as per the Product Description in Appendix A, and additional guidance provided in the PRINCE2 manual?'

7.4 Use of true statements in a question

When the expression '**true statements**' is used in a question, **no evaluation of whether the statements are consistent with the scenario or additional information is required**.

In the above example there is no need in option A and C to check the scenario to see if the project is being funded from the business marketing budget or that the costs are £26.5k. As it is known from the question header that the statement is true, the assessment required is whether, according to the recommended PRINCE2 content of Business Case, the 'costs heading' is the correct place for recording this information.

Each of the following 5 questions includes a number of **true statements** about the project but, only **2** statements are appropriate entries for that heading of the Business Case.		
1		Which **2** statements should be recorded under the **costs** heading?
	A	The project will be funded from the business marketing budget.
	B	No project cost information can be provided until the Project Plan has been approved.
	C	Project costs are estimated to be a total of £26.5k.
	D	The cost of printing and distribution will be recorded in the production cost forecast.
	E	10 further orders with an average profit of £2k will deliver a benefit of £20k in the first year.

7.5 Use of 'according to PRINCE2'

The expression 'according to PRINCE2' is used to stress that the question is purely theoretical and does not require evaluation of scenario information.

8 Using the Answer Booklet

The Answer Booklet will be read electronically and the results generated by computer. It is therefore essential that candidates follow the instructions given and mark their answers accordingly. Failure to do so may lead to delay and, in some cases, answers being void.

All answers are given by the candidate filling in 'ovals' that relate to their chosen response, as shown in the figure below.

Example of format used in Answer Booklet

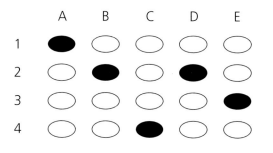

The oval must be filled in **in pencil, not pen**. If a pen is used, the answers will not be marked.

Acceptable ways to complete the answer sheets are either by completely filling in the oval, or drawing a horizontal line through the centre of the oval. Any other method, including ticks or crosses, is not acceptable and will not be marked.

If a candidate wishes to change their answer during the exam, the incorrect answer should be erased completely and the correct answer indicated. If more than one answer is given by the candidate, and the question requires only one answer, the question will score zero.

9 Re-registration exam

The re-registration exam will follow the same format as the practitioner exam but the Question Booklet will contain three questions, giving a total of 36 marks, to be answered within one hour. The pass mark is 20 (55%). Each question will test one of the syllabus areas. A maximum of one process area will be tested in each paper.

All other guidance is applicable to both the PRINCE2 practitioner and re-registration examinations.

4.5 SAMPLE PAPER

Note that the material that follows (Scenario Booklet, Question Booklet, Answer Booklet and Rationale) has been taken from the APM Group's document: EX02 PRINCE2 2009 Sample Practitioner Paper 1 V1.6.

The Practitioner Examination

EX02
SCENARIO BOOKLET

This is a 2.5-hour objective test. This booklet contains the Project Scenario upon which this exam paper is based. All questions are contained within the *Question Booklet*.

Additional information is provided within this *Scenario Booklet* for a number of questions. Where reference should be made to additional information, this is clearly stated within the question to which it is relevant. All information provided within a question must only be applied to that question.

Each of the nine questions is worth 12 marks, giving a maximum of 108 marks in the paper. The pass mark is 55% (59 marks). Within each question the syllabus area to which the question refers is clearly stated. The exam is to be taken with the support of the PRINCE2 Manual only, i.e. no material other than the *Question Booklet*, the *Scenario Booklet*, the *Answer Booklet* and the PRINCE2 Manual is to be used.

Candidate Number: ....

PROJECT SCENARIO
Calendar Project

There has been a reduction in order numbers at the MNO Manufacturing Company due in part to the increased marketing activities of its competitors. To help counter this, it has been decided to create a promotional calendar for next year for all its current and prospective customers.

The end product of this project will be a prepared calendar pack, ready for printing. The design of the calendar will be similar to one sent out previously, and must reflect the company image as described in the existing corporate branding standards. Another project is currently producing a new company logo which is to be printed on each page of the promotional calendar. The prepared calendar pack will consist of:

- Monthly calendar displays – correctly showing all public holidays and new company logo
- Selected photos – 12 professionally-produced photos, showing different members of staff
- Selected paper and selected envelope – for printing and mailing the calendar
- Chosen label design integrating new company logo – competition to be held as part of this project
- List of customers – names and addresses of customers to whom the calendar will be sent

The project is currently in initiation and will have two further stages:

- Stage 2 will include the activities to:
  - create the customer list using information from the Accounts and Marketing departments
  - confirm compliance with the Data Protection Act
  - design of the monthly calendar displays – this will be done by the internal creative team
  - select and appoint a professional photographer
  - gather photo design ideas from previous project and agree photo session schedule
  - prepare a production cost forecast
  - select paper and envelope
- Stage 3 will include the activities to:
  - take and select the professional photos
  - hold the label design competition and choose the label design
  - assemble the prepared calendar pack.

A production cost forecast, based on the options and costs for the paper, envelope, printing and mailing of the calendar is to be produced in stage 2. However, the actual production and distribution of the calendars is not within the scope of this project. The production cost forecast will be reviewed by the Project Board to determine whether the project should continue.

It is now 05 October and the prepared calendar pack must be delivered to the print company by 30 November, to enable printing and distribution of the calendar in time for Christmas. The cost of the activities to develop the specialist products and the cost of the project management activities are estimated to be £20k. There is a project time tolerance of +1 week/-2 weeks and a project cost tolerance of +£6k/-£6k. A change budget of £500 has been allocated but there is no risk budget.

Question 1: Business Case Theme – Additional Information

During the initiation stage the Project Manager met with the Marketing Director to find out more about the requirements of the promotional calendar and recorded the following notes:

There has been a reduction in the order numbers at MNO Manufacturing due in part to the increased marketing activities of its competitors. 10% of customers have not re-ordered in this financial year and staff morale is poor. A number of skilled staff have left as a result and replacement staff have not been recruited due to the reduced operation. If the project is successful, a recruitment campaign will be required to fill the existing staff vacancies and there may be a requirement for additional staff. Operational costs are likely to increase because skilled staff are expensive and difficult to find.

In financial terms, there were a total of 1,500 orders in the last financial year, each with an average profit of £2k. The Marketing department believes that sending a promotional calendar to our current and prospective customers would increase orders by at least 10% with a minimum of 10 further orders from the list of prospective customers within 12 months from the date of distribution.

The Marketing Director will be funding the project from the business marketing budget. She believes that the effect of a good company image portrayed by a successful calendar would last into a second year. She has forecast the same increase in orders for a second year and predicts that the annual employee satisfaction survey will show a measurable improvement in staff morale.

A number of alternatives were explored, including:

- 20% discount for all repeat customers – not cost-effective and very short term
- A promotional calendar as a free Christmas gift – would target current and prospective customers and the benefits would last into a second year
- A series of TV and press advertisements – was too expensive
- A direct mail shot to all customers – benefit would be short term
- Creation of an internet website – would not suit all customers

The calendar is seen as the favoured option, as long as the company's competitors do not increase their marketing activity. Whilst the Marketing department wants a very high quality, glossy product, the project management team must be aware of the cost this will incur.

Question 2: Organization Theme – Additional Information

Chief Executive Officer (CEO): He started the company 25 years ago and knows his job very well. He injured his leg two years ago which has restricted his visits to the engineering area. As CEO he has an overall perspective of the business strategic requirements and the authority to commit resources as required.

Marketing Director: She has been with the company for three years, following a successful career with a publicity company. She has the ability to represent the needs of the business, particularly as this is a marketing project. She has the authority to commit the annual business marketing budget, from which the project will be funded, as she sees appropriate. She will be responsible for monitoring the expected benefits of the calendar, in particular the improvement of the company's image.

Engineering Manager: He has been responsible for many engineering innovations in the company and is still as keen and energetic as the day he started. Whilst he will not be part of the project team, his staff will feature in the photos for the promotional calendar.

Central Records: This group of five staff looks after all company records and document control. They now maintain all project files.

Bright Lights: This is the local office supplies company. It supplies all the stationery and office equipment needs of the company and will supply the stationery for this project.

Portraits Ltd: This is a professional photographic company with a number of excellent photographers and a history of successful work. This company has been selected to take the photos for the company calendar. It has yet to be decided which of the photographers to use.

Question 3: Quality Theme – Additional Information

Extract from the Project Product Description (with errors)

Composition	1. Monthly calendar displays
	2. 100gsm glossy paper
	3. Full colour
	4. Selected envelope
	5. Chosen label design
	6. List of customers
	7. Selected photos
	8. Photo session schedule
Derivation	9. New company logo design
	10. Previous calendar designs
	11. Internal creative team
	12. Production cost forecast
Development skills required	13. Photographer
	14. Internal creative team
	15. Printer
Customer's quality expectations	16. Professional photos
	17. 10% more calendars should be printed than required to allow for any late additions to the list of customers
	18. Compliance with applicable corporate standards
	19. The calendar should reflect the company image as described in the corporate branding standards
	20. The calendar will increase orders by at least 10% with a minimum of 10 further orders from the list of prospective customers within 12 months

continues

Acceptance criteria	21. Appearance – each photo should be sufficiently attractive and humorous that the customer wants to display it
	22. Appearance – new company logo promotes strong image
	23. Security – complies with Data Protection Act
	24. Accuracy – public holidays match the list supplied by Marketing on 01 November

Question 4: Starting up a Project + Initiating a Project Processes – Additional Information

Extract from the Communication Management Strategy

The project information in the table below is **true**, but it may not be recorded under the correct heading or be in the correct document.

Introduction	1. This document contains details of how the project management team will send information to individuals working on the Calendar project, and receive information from them.
Communication procedure	2. See MNO Manufacturing Company standards for all internal company communications.
Tools and techniques	3. Use the staff newsletter to launch the label design competition and to promote the chosen label design.
	4. Using the number of responses to the label design competition as a measure, report fortnightly to the Project Board on the effectiveness of the staff newsletter as a vehicle for communication.
	5. Use the company website to advertise the promotional calendar to customers.
Records	6. A record should be maintained for each product of the project. As a minimum this should show the project name, product name, product title, and version number.
	7. External email and correspondence relating to the Calendar project should be recorded electronically in the project folder.
	8. Information received in hard copy should, where possible, be scanned and filed as above.
Timing of communication activities	9. At the end of each stage, audit and report on the performance of the communication methods being used.
	10. Highlight Reports to be provided to appropriate stakeholders, at the frequency defined in each Stage Plan.
Stakeholder analysis: Interested parties	11. Photographer.
	12. Print company.
Stakeholder analysis: Information needs for each interested party	13. Weekly updates will be provided by email to the individual producing the staff newsletter.
	14. Engineering Manager is to be consulted when preparing the photo session schedule.

Question 5: Risk Theme – Additional Information

A photographer from Portraits Ltd, a professional photographic company, has taken on the role of Team Manager after taking some time to understand the requirements of the project. A contract for their services has been set up and is being monitored by the Purchasing Manager and a Work Package has been agreed. This contract specifies that the photographer must arrange a meeting with the Engineering Manager to establish a schedule for the photo sessions to minimize the impact on the Engineering staff. This meeting should have occurred by now.

The Engineering Manager was made aware of this requirement but when asked he reported that he has received no communication from the photographer. The Project Manager has tried to call the photographer and has had no response. The Project Manager believes there is a risk that Portraits Ltd are overbooking work and prioritizing other clients' work. If Portraits Ltd do not deliver on schedule the project will be delayed and the expected benefits will be reduced.

The contract is to be reviewed and Portraits Ltd reminded of their agreement.

Question 6: Plans Theme – Additional Information

Product Summary

A list of customers will be collated. This will use existing information from the Accounts department about current customers, and existing information from the Marketing department about prospective customers.

Using the tariff of mailing costs available from the Post Office, a production cost forecast will be produced to allow the CEO and the Marketing Director to decide whether to continue with the project. If they decide to continue, they will give the approval to launch the internal label design competition. Competition rules will be required to communicate details of the competition to the staff. The chosen label design will then be selected from the competition entries.

The photos for the calendar must be based on existing photo design ideas available from the Marketing department. The selected photos will be chosen from these. Monthly calendar displays will be created to show the required layout of each page.

Product Breakdown Structure (contains errors)

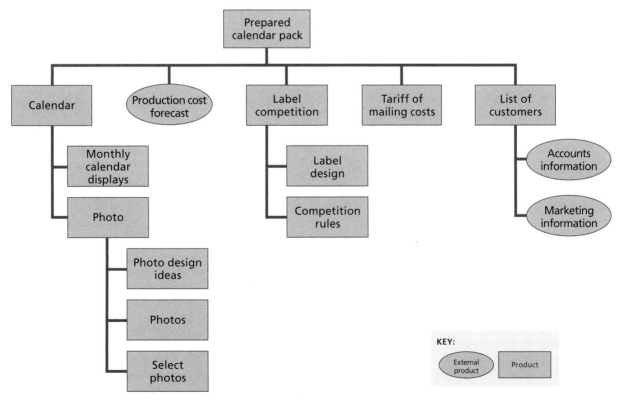

Question 6: Plans Theme – Additional Information

Extract from Stage Plan for stage 3

(All entries are **true statements** but may not be shown under the correct heading or in the correct document.)

Plan description	1. Stage 3 is the final stage of the project and will deliver the photos, the label design competition entries, the winning label design and the prepared calendar pack.
Plan prerequisites	2. Increase in orders and improved company image.
	3. The production cost forecast must be acceptable to the Project Board if the photography and label design competition are to go ahead.
	4. The customer list is accurate and complete.
External dependencies	5. A separate project has been reviewing the company's branding. The company logo, required for the label design competition, is being updated. The new company logo is to be supplied by the other project in two weeks' time.
	6. Customer details will be supplied from the Accounts department and the Marketing department customer databases for the customer list.
	7. The label design must contain the new company logo.
Planning assumptions	8. A suitable entry will be received from the label design competition.
	9. The photo session schedule created two weeks ago correctly reflects the availability of the engineering staff.
	10. Each photo must feature different members of the Engineering team.
Monitoring and control	11. The Project Plan is to be updated with actuals throughout the stage.
	12. A Highlight Report will be created for corporate/programme management every two weeks.
	13. The Stage Plan will be reviewed at the end of each day, to assess forecast against actuals.
	14. Product Status Accounts will be produced by Project Support, at the request of the Project Manager, to summarize current and historical data concerning each of the project's products.
Budgets	15. Cost £5k for specialist products
	16. Time 4 weeks
	17. Risk £0

The Practitioner Examination

EX02
QUESTION BOOKLET

Candidate Number: ....

SYLLABUS AREAS COVERED:

Question 1 – Business Case Theme

Question 2 – Organization Theme

Question 3 – Quality Theme

Question 4 – Starting up a Project + Initiating a Project Processes

Question 5 – Risk Theme

Question 6 – Plans Theme

Question 7 – Progress Theme

Question 8 – Change Theme

Question 9 – Directing a Project + Managing a Stage Boundary + Closing a Project Processes

QUESTION NUMBER 1

Syllabus Area   Business Case Theme

Syllabus Area	Question Number	Part	Marks
Business Case Theme	1	A	7

Using the Project Scenario and the additional information provided for this question in the *Scenario Booklet*, answer the following 7 questions.

Each question provides a list of **true statements** about the Calendar project, but only 2 statements are appropriate entries for that heading of the Business Case.

Remember to limit your answers to the number of selections requested in each question.

1	Which **2** statements should be recorded under the **Reasons** heading?
	A The Marketing department believes that sending a promotional calendar to current and prospective customers will increase orders by at least 10%.
	B 10% of customers have not re-ordered in this financial year.
	C 1,500 orders are expected, each with an average profit of £2k.
	D The Marketing department believes that the effect of a good company image, portrayed by a successful calendar, will last into a second year.
	E MNO Manufacturing is experiencing a fall in orders due in part to the increased marketing activities of its competitors.
2	Which **2** statements should be recorded under the **Business options** heading?
	A Produce a promotional calendar as a free Christmas gift to current and prospective customers.
	B Use a professional photographer to create the photographs for the calendar.
	C Create the photographs for the calendar internally.
	D Outsource the creation of the calendar to a professional marketing company.
	E Do nothing.

Question Number 1 continued

3	Which **2** statements should be recorded under the **Expected benefits** heading?
	A Increase orders by at least 10% with a minimum of 10 further orders from the list of prospective customers within 12 months.
	B It will be similar to calendars sent out in previous years
	C The Marketing department believes that the benefits of a good company image, as portrayed by a successful calendar, will last into a second year and bring the same increase in orders.
	D The calendar will contain photos of both staff and company products.
	E The Marketing department want a very high quality, glossy product as they believe this will be more appealing to customers.
4	Which **2** statements should be recorded under the **Expected dis-benefits** heading?
	A A high quality, glossy product will involve additional costs.
	B Individuals in the engineering team who are not selected to appear in the calendar photographs will become de-motivated.
	C The calendar may not result in the expected 10% increase in orders.
	D Because the Calendar project is a priority for the MNO Manufacturing Company, the delivery of other projects within the Marketing department will be delayed.
	E The calendar may not result in the 10 further orders from the list of prospective customers in 12 months.
5	Which **2** statements should be recorded under the **Timescale** heading?
	A Benefits will be lost if the project is not completed on time.
	B A recruitment campaign to fill the existing staff vacancies will need to take place in the next 12 months.
	C Additional 10% increase in orders in year two.
	D The prepared calendar pack must be delivered by the first week in December.
	E The print company requires a 2-week notification period of the calendar pack delivery.
6	Which **2** statements should be recorded under the **Costs** heading?
	A The MNO marketing budget this year is £120k.
	B The project will be funded from the business marketing budget.
	C 10 further orders with an average profit of £2k will deliver a benefit of £20k in the first year.
	D The new company logo is estimated to cost £4k.
	E Project costs are estimated to be a total of £26.5k.

7	Which **2** statements correctly define a Business Case risk which should be recorded under the **Major risks** heading?
	A Operational costs will increase as a result of the recruitment campaign.
	B The prepared calendar pack is to be delivered to the printers by the first week in December.
	C If the calendar quality is poor customers will not use it, creating the reverse effect and reducing orders further.
	D If any competitors launch a calendar at the same time this will reduce the impact of the MNO calendar and benefits will be reduced.
	E Staff morale may improve as a result of the promotional calendar.

Syllabus Area	Question Number	Part	Marks
Business Case Theme	1	B	5

Using the Project Scenario and the additional information provided for this question in the *Scenario Booklet*, answer the following question.

Lines 1 to 5 in the table below consist of an assertion statement and a reason statement. For each line identify the appropriate option, from options A to E, that applies. Each option can be used once, more than once or not at all.

Option	Assertion	Reason	
A	True	True	AND the reason explains the assertion
B	True	True	BUT the reason does not explain the assertion
C	True	False	
D	False	True	
E	False	False	

	Assertion		Reason
1	If the calendar solution is changed there should be a review of, and possible changes to, the Business Case.	BECAUSE	The Business Case includes options for the delivery of the chosen solution.
2	The Business Case will no longer be viable if the prepared calendar pack is only available for printing in the first week of December.	BECAUSE	The Business Case is no longer viable if stage tolerances are exceeded during the project.

Question Number 1 continued

3	The fact that the project's aim is to try to counter the fall in orders should be documented in the Project Brief.	BECAUSE	The outline Business Case contains the reasons why the project is needed and forms part of the Project Brief.
4	The Benefits Review Plan should include an assessment in 12 months' time of the increase in orders.	BECAUSE	The Benefits Review Plan contains details of benefits reviews to be conducted during the project.
5	The expected improvement in staff morale should NOT be recorded as a benefit in the Business Case.	BECAUSE	Only those benefits that can be measured in financial terms should be defined in the Business Case.

QUESTION NUMBER 2

Syllabus Area   Organization Theme

Syllabus Area	Question Number	Part	Marks
Organization Theme	2	A	7

The following 7 questions include a number of **true statements** about an individual from the project organization. Only 2 statements explain why, in the context of roles and responsibilities within a PRINCE2 organization structure, the individual is a suitable candidate for that role.

Remember to limit your answers to the number of selections requested in each question.

1	Which **2** statements explain why the Marketing Director should be appointed as the Executive for this project?
	A She has been with the company for three years.
	B She previously had a successful career in publicity.
	C She is able to represent the needs of MNO Manufacturing.
	D She has authority to commit the marketing budget, from which the project will be funded.
	E She requires more experience working with the engineering industry.
2	Which **2** statements explain why the CEO should be appointed as the Executive for this project?
	A He started the company 25 years ago.
	B He knows his job very well.
	C He restricts his visits to the engineering area.
	D He has the authority to commit resources as required.
	E He has an overall perspective of the business's strategic requirements.

Question Number 2 continued

3	Which **2** statements explain why the Marketing Director should be appointed as a Senior User for this project?
	A She can represent the Marketing department.
	B She previously had a successful career in publicity.
	C It is the Marketing department who will deliver the benefits of this project.
	D The project will be funded from the business marketing budget.
	E A number of the products will be produced by the Sales department and the Marketing department.
4	Which **2** statements explain why the Sales Manager should be appointed as a Senior User for this project?
	A He joined the company last year with huge enthusiasm.
	B He would like to move into the Marketing department in the future and sees this as an opportunity to work closely with the Marketing Director.
	C The launch of a company calendar will impact the Sales department.
	D He reports directly to the Marketing Director.
	E He is able to represent current and prospective customer interests.
5	Which **2** statements explain why the Purchasing Manager should be appointed as a Senior Supplier for this project?
	A He is responsible for the organization's procurement activities.
	B He is responsible for the performance of supplier contracts.
	C He was an engineer and worked in that area before taking up his current position.
	D He can influence the external supplier's Business Case.
	E He is not appropriate for the role of Executive or Senior User.
6	Which **2** statements explain why the Sales Manager should be appointed as User Assurance for this project?
	A He joined the company last year with huge enthusiasm and is keen to increase sales.
	B He can provide an evaluation of the potential impact the calendar will have on sales.
	C He is able to advise on suitable stakeholder engagement of current and prospective customers.
	D He would like to move into the Marketing department in the future and sees this as an opportunity to work closely with the Marketing Director.
	E He can resolve any conflict in requirements between the Sales department and the Marketing department.

7	Which **2** statements explain why Central Records should be appointed as Project Support for this project?
	A They control the receipt, identification, versions, storage and issue of all project products.
	B They already exist within the organization and have many years of experience.
	C They will ensure compliance with all company policies and procedures.
	D They perform a quality assurance function across all projects.
	E They have knowledge of the organizational standards that will be applicable to the project.

Syllabus Area	Question Number	Part	Marks
Organization Theme	2	B	5

Using the additional information provided for this question in the *Scenario Booklet*, answer the following question.

Lines 1 to 5 in the table below consist of an assertion statement and a reason statement. For each line identify the appropriate option, from options A to E, that applies. Each option can be used once, more than once or not at all.

Option	Assertion	Reason	
A	True	True	AND the reason explains the assertion
B	True	True	BUT the reason does not explain the assertion
C	True	False	
D	False	True	
E	False	False	

	Assertion		Reason
1	The Executive role should be shared by the CEO and the Marketing Director	BECAUSE	The Executive is responsible for securing the funding for the project
2	The Senior User role should be shared by the Marketing Director and the Engineering Manager.	BECAUSE	Those who provide specialist resources to the project development teams should perform a Senior User role.
3	Although Bright Lights and Portraits Ltd are suppliers, they CANNOT both perform a Senior Supplier role on this project.	BECAUSE	When the Senior Supplier role is shared between two suppliers, one of the suppliers must be internal to the business.

Question Number 2 continued

4	A single member of Central Records should NOT perform both a Project Support and a Project Assurance role on this project.	BECAUSE	It is necessary to keep Project Support and Project Assurance responsibilities separate.
5	The Engineering Manager should be included in the Communication Management Strategy.	BECAUSE	The Communication Management Strategy describes the communication tools to be used.

QUESTION NUMBER 3

Syllabus Area   Quality Theme

Syllabus Area	Question Number	Part	Marks
Quality Theme	3	A	3

Column 1 is a list of objectives. For each objective in Column 1, select from Column 2 the quality activity that addresses it. Each selection from Column 2 can be used once, more than once or not at all.

	Column 1		Column 2
1	Understanding the customer's quality expectations.	A	Quality assurance
2	Approval of the project's products.	B	Quality control
3	Confirmation that corporate management standards and policies are being adhered to.	C	Quality planning

Syllabus Area	Question Number	Part	Marks
Quality Theme	3	B	4

An address label is required for the envelope. The design of the label will be selected from entries to an internal label design competition. The winning label design will be included in the prepared calendar pack given to the printing company. The label should be half the size of the selected envelope (+5%/-5%), and use an attractive, large font for the customer's name and address. The new company logo must be integrated into the label design. The Project Board will be asked to review all entries and select the winning label design.

The information in Column 1 may be entered in the Product Description for the chosen label design. Column 2 is a list of the quality headings (excluding Quality Method) in a Product Description. For each entry in Column 1 decide if it should be included in the Product Description headings shown and select the heading from Column 2 under which it should be recorded.

Each selection from Column 2 can be used once, more than once or not at all.

Question Number 3 continued

	Column 1	Column 2
1	Half the size of the selected envelope.	A Not included
2	Attractive large font.	B Quality criteria
3	Project Board.	C Quality tolerance
4	+5%/-5% of the required label size.	D Quality skills required
		E Quality responsibilities

Syllabus Area	Question Number	Part	Marks
Quality Theme	3	C	5

Using the Project Scenario and the additional information provided for this question in the *Scenario Booklet*, answer the following 5 questions about the Project Product Description.

Remember to limit your answers to the number of selections requested in each question.

1	Which **2** statements apply to the **Composition** section?
	A Amend entry 2 to 'Selected paper'.
	B Delete entry 3 because this is NOT a major product to be delivered by this project.
	C Move entry 6 to **Derivation** because this product already exists.
	D Delete entry 7 because these will be produced by the photographer.
	E Add 'Calendars distributed to customers'.
2	Which **2** statements apply to the **Derivation** section?
	A Move entry 9 to **Composition** because this is within the scope of the project.
	B Delete entry 10 because this is NOT a source product for this project.
	C Delete entry 11 as this is already correctly shown under **Development Skills required**.
	D Move entry 12 to **Composition**, because this is within the scope of this project.
	E Add 'Professional photographer'.

3	Which **2** statements apply to the **Development skills required** section?
	A Move entry 13 to **Composition** because the appointment of the photographer is within the scope of this project.
	B Move entry 13 to **Derivation** because this is a source of information for this project.
	C Delete entry 14 because this skill is NOT required within this project.
	D Delete entry 15 because this skill is NOT required within this project.
	E Add 'Knowledge of Data Protection Act'.
4	Which **2** statements apply to the **Customer's quality expectations** section?
	A Delete entry 16 because this should be shown on the Product Description for the photos.
	B Delete entry 17 because this is beyond the scope of this project.
	C Delete entry 18 because standards should NOT be shown here.
	D Delete entry 19 because this should appear in the Product Description for the calendar and not the Project Product Description.
	E Delete entry 20 because this is an expected benefit and should be recorded in the Business Case.
5	Which **2** statements apply to the **Acceptance criteria** section?
	A Amend entry 21 to 'Appearance – 12 photos each showing different members of staff'.
	B Move entry 21 to **Composition** because the photos are part of the final product.
	C Delete entry 22 because the development of the new company logo is not within the scope of the Calendar project.
	D Move entry 23 to **Derivation** because the Data Protection Act already exists.
	E Delete entry 24 because this is NOT a suitable acceptance criteria for this project.

QUESTION NUMBER 4

Syllabus Area   Starting up a Project + Initiating a Project Processes

Syllabus Area	Question Number	Part	Marks
Starting up a Project + Initiating a Project Processes	4	A	5

Using the Project Scenario, select the appropriate response to each of the following 5 questions which have been raised by the Project Board.

The project is now at the end of the initiation stage. Having decided that the Calendar project is a relatively simple project, the Project Manager combined the Starting Up a Project process and the Initiating a Project process. No Project Brief has been produced, instead the Project Manager used the project mandate to produce a simple Project Initiation Document (PID). The PID includes the Business Case, a product checklist and several Product Descriptions, including the Project Product Description. Short sections are also included for each of the strategies and the controls to be applied. The Project Manager has elected to use the Daily Log to record all risks, issues, lessons and quality results.

After the initiation stage there will be two further stages during which a small number of Work Packages will be authorized. While these are being managed, the Project Manager will hold regular checkpoints, which will support the production of weekly Highlight Reports to the Project Board.

1	There is no project schedule in the Project Initiation Documentation. How can project progress be tracked without a schedule to track against?
A	This is an error as a Gantt chart or some form of time line, where actuals will be recorded and tracked against the planned schedule of delivery, is mandatory.
B	Progress will be recorded and tracked using the product checklist, with the planned and actual quality management activities captured in the Daily Log.
C	With a clear end date of 30 November, and a small number of Work Packages, the Project Board should track project progress using individual Team Plans.
2	There is no Project Brief. How can there be a common understanding of the desired outcomes for the prepared calendar pack?
A	The simple Project Initiation Documentation contains the Quality Management Strategy. This contains details of the acceptance criteria for this project.
B	The Project Brief should have been produced and approved before the project progressed into the initiation stage.
C	The simple Project Initiation Documentation contains the Project Product Description. This contains details of the customer's quality expectations.

3	There is no mention of any Stage Plans, yet there are two further stages proposed. How will this be resolved?
	A It is appropriate for the Calendar project to be run as two further stages as there is a key decision to be made at the end of stage 2. Stage Plans will be produced.
	B Whilst the activities are divided into two further stages, there is no reason why the Calendar project should use stages. The project will therefore be run as a single-stage project and the activities will be added to the initiation Stage Plan.
	C There will be three Stage Plans, the two management stages plus an additional stage to plan and complete the activities of the Closing a Project process.
4	No separate Benefits Review Plan has been developed. When will the schedule of benefit reviews be recorded?
	A The Benefits Review Plan will be created at the end of stage 2, when the production cost forecast has been approved and the Business Case updated with the expected benefits of the project.
	B The activities to measure the success of the project outcomes in realizing their benefits will be defined at the end of the project, during the Closing a Project process.
	C As a simple project, it is acceptable to incorporate the Benefits Review Plan within the Project Plan during initiation.
5	Without a Risk Register, how can project risks, the progress of risk actions taken to date and the current status of residual risks be measured?
	A The Daily Log was correctly used to monitor risks during the Starting up a Project process. It will be used to capture all risks, actions, decisions, assumptions.
	B It was not appropriate to use the Daily Log to capture all risks and issues during the Starting up a Project process. Separate registers should have been set up for risks, issues and lessons learned. This will now be done.
	C In a simple project, the Project Initiation Documentation (PID) should contain a register for recording risk information and monitoring project risks throughout the delivery stages. The register will now be added to the PID.

Syllabus Area	Question Number	Part	Marks
Starting up a Project + Initiating a Project Processes	4	B	7

Using the Project Scenario and additional information provided for this question in the *Scenario Booklet*, answer the following 7 questions.

Each of the following questions provides a number of changes which may or may not be required to the extract from the Communication Management Strategy provided in the additional information.

Question Number 4 continued

1	Which statement applies to the **Introduction** section?
	A No change to entry 1 because this shows the purpose and content of this document.
	B Amend entry 1 to read 'This document contains the controls and reporting to be established for the project management team'.
	C Amend entry 1 to read 'This document contains the means and frequency of communication between the project management team, the print company and other external parties.'
2	Which statement applies to the **Communication procedure** section?
	A No change to entry 2 because this is a sufficient description of the process required.
	B Amend entry 2 to include MNO Manufacturing Company standards for both internal and external company communications.
	C Delete entry 2 because only variations from the MNO Manufacturing Company standards should be recorded here.
3	Which statement applies to the **Tools and techniques** section?
	A Delete entry 3 because the activities required to create the products should be documented in the relevant plan(s).
	B Move entry 4 to **Reporting** because this describes a report on the performance of the Communication procedures used.
	C Delete entry 5 because the customers are not within the scope of this project
4	Which statement applies to the **Records** section?
	A Move entry 6 to the **Configuration Management Strategy** because it defines the identification scheme for the project's products.
	B Move entry 7 to **Communication procedure** because it refers to the method to be used for communicating to external parties.
	C Move entry 8 to **Tools and techniques** because it refers to a filing technique.
5	Which statement applies to the **Timing of communication activities** section?
	A Delete entry 9 because activities for controlling the project should be planned as part of **Project controls** in the Project Initiation Documentation.
	B No change to entry 9 because it describes the timing of performance reports.
	C Delete entry 10 because Highlight Reports are a Project Board control, the frequency of which should be recorded in the **Project controls** section of the Project Initiation Documentation.

6	Which statement applies to the **Stakeholder analysis: Interested parties** section?
	A Add 'Internal Creative Team'.
	B Delete entry 11 because the photographer is internal to the project management team.
	C Delete entry 12 because the printing of the calendars is outside of the scope of this project.
7	Which statement applies to the **Stakeholder analysis: Information needs for each interested party** section?
	A Delete entry 13 because the activity to provide the weekly updates should be scheduled in the relevant Stage Plan.
	B Move entry 13 to **Tools and techniques** because it describes the method to be used to communicate to the individual producing the staff newsletter.
	C Delete entry 14 because this relates to the development of a particular product and should be recorded under **Development interfaces** within the relevant Work Package.

QUESTION NUMBER 5

Syllabus Area   Risk Theme

Syllabus Area	Question Number	Part	Marks
Risk Theme	5	A	6

The project is now in stage 2. The Project Manager has heard about the possibility of a competitor also producing a calendar to be delivered earlier than the target date for this project. There is a threat that the early release of a competitor's calendar may weaken the impact of the MNO Manufacturing Company calendar, thereby reducing the anticipated benefits of the Calendar project.

Column 1 contains a number of risk responses identified by the Project Manager following an assessment of this risk. Column 2 contains a list of threat response types. For each risk response in Column 1, select from Column 2 the type of response it represents. Each option from Column 2 can be used once, more than once or not at all.

	Column 1	Column 2
1	Record the risk in the Risk Register and monitor the situation.	A Avoid
		B Reduce
2	Decide not to compete and cancel the project.	C Fallback
3	Bring the target date of this project forward.	D Transfer
4	Wait for confirmation of the rival's calendar and, if required, include additional gifts with the calendar as an extra incentive.	E Accept
		F Share
5	Carry on with the project as planned on the basis that the MNO Manufacturing Company calendar is believed to be of better quality.	
6	Add a unique reference number to every calendar and hold a prize draw each month.	

Syllabus Area	Question Number	Part	Marks
Risk Theme	5	B	6

Using the additional information provided for this question in the *Scenario Booklet*, answer the following question.

Lines 1 to 6 in the table below consist of an assertion statement and a reason statement. For each line identify the appropriate option, from options A to E, that applies. Each option can be used once, more than once or not at all.

Option	Assertion	Reason	
A	True	True	AND the reason explains the assertion
B	True	True	BUT the reason does not explain the assertion
C	True	False	
D	False	True	
E	False	False	

	Assertion		Reason
1	The Engineering Manager should have raised the fact that there has been no contact with the photographer as an issue.	BECAUSE	Any forecast to exceed the agreed stage tolerances should be escalated to the Project Board.
2	As the person monitoring the contract, the Purchasing Manager would be an appropriate owner for the risk.	BECAUSE	The risk owner is responsible for the management of the implementation of any selected responses to address the threat or maximize the opportunity
3	The photographer should have raised any concerns about their availability for the work as a risk before accepting the Work Package.	BECAUSE	A separate Risk Register should be created for each Work Package to monitor specialist risks associated with the creation of specialist products.
4	If estimation of the risk shows that it is likely to impact upon time, the Project Manager will need to raise an Issue Report.	BECAUSE	When the impact of a risk has been identified, an Issue Report will be required to implement any agreed risk actions.
5	Regular Checkpoint Reports from the photographer will help the Project Manager manage the risk.	BECAUSE	Checkpoint Reports should provide early warning of any delay in the photographer's work.

Question Number 5 continued

6	As a Work Package has been agreed with the photographer, the Project Manager needs to take no further action on the risk because the photographer should have it under control.	BECAUSE	When selecting the most appropriate risk response to take, the best option is usually the least expensive.

QUESTION NUMBER 6

Syllabus Area   Plans Theme

Syllabus Area	Question Number	Part	Marks
Plans Theme	6	A	7

Using the Product Summary and Product Breakdown Structure provided as additional information for this question in the *Scenario Booklet*, answer the following question.

Column 1 is a list of some of the entries in the product breakdown structure. Determine whether each entry in Column 1 has been correctly shown in the Product Breakdown Structure. Select from Column 2 the appropriate statement that correctly describes that entry. Each selection from Column 2 can be used once, more than once or not at all.

	Column 1	Column 2
1	Production cost forecast	A External product incorrectly shown
2	Tariff of mailing costs	B Internal product incorrectly shown as an external product
3	Photo design ideas	C NOT a product
4	Accounts information	D Correctly shown entry
5	Monthly calendar displays	
6	Label design	
7	Select photos	

Question Number 6 continued

Syllabus Area	Question Number	Part	Marks
Plans Theme	6	B	5

Using the Project Scenario and the Extract from Stage Plan for stage 3 provided as additional information for this question in the *Scenario Booklet*, answer the following 5 questions.

The Stage Plan for stage 3 has been produced.

The Engineering Manager insists that there are to be no interruptions to operations whilst photographs are being taken of the engineering staff performing their everyday duties and operating machinery. Two weeks ago the professional photographer produced the photo session schedule based on the operational staff schedule. The operational staff schedule is produced weekly and maintained by the Engineering Manager.

None of the £500 change budget has been used to date and this is available for the stage.

Remember to limit your answers to the number of selections requested in each question.

1	Which **2** statements apply to the **Plan prerequisites** section?
	A Delete entry 2 because these are project benefits not prerequisites of the stage.
	B Delete entry 3 because the production cost forecast is a deliverable of stage 2, not a prerequisite for stage 3.
	C Delete entry 4 because the customer list is a deliverable of stage 2, not a prerequisite for stage 3.
	D Add 'Engineering team must be made available for photos'.
	E Add 'Compliance with the Data Protection Act'.
2	Which **2** statements apply to the **External dependencies** section?
	A Delete entry 5 because the new company logo is being delivered by a separate project and will be detailed in the plans for that project.
	B Move entry 5 to **Plan prerequisites** because the new company logo will influence the label designs.
	C Move entry 5 to **Plan description** because the new company logo will be delivered during stage 3.
	D Delete entry 6 because the customer details were used in stage 2 to create the customer list.
	E Delete entry 7 because it should be shown in the Product Description for the label design.

3	Which **2** statements apply to the **Planning assumptions** section?
	A No change to entry 8 because this cannot be confirmed until all of the label design entries have been received and an assessment made.
	B Move entry 8 to **External dependencies** because the label designs are created outside of the scope of the project.
	C Delete entry 9 because the photo session schedule should have been approved as part of stage 2.
	D Move entry 9 to **External dependencies** because the photo session schedule is created by the professional photographer.
	E Delete entry 10 because the inclusion of different members from the Engineering team in each photo should be shown in the Product Description for the photos.
4	Which **2** statements apply to the **Monitoring and control** section?
	A Delete entry 11 because this relates to the monitoring and controlling of the Project Plan, not the Stage Plan.
	B Delete entry 12 because it is about the information needs of corporate/programme management rather than how the stage will be monitored.
	C Move entry 12 because the Highlight Reports are deliverables of this stage and should be shown under **Product descriptions**.
	D Delete entry 13 because this is part of the Controlling a Stage process.
	E Delete entry 14 because the Product Status Account is NOT an ad-hoc report. It is produced at the end of each stage to identify any variations between planned status, reported status and actual status of the stage's products.
5	Which **2** statements apply to the **Budgets** section?
	A Amend entry 15 because it should also include the cost of management activities.
	B Delete entry 16 because timescales should NOT be shown under the heading of budgets.
	C Delete entry 17 because the risk budget should be shown in the Risk Management Strategy.
	D Add 'Change budget – £500'.
	E Add 'Cost tolerance – +£6k/-£6k'

QUESTION NUMBER 7

Syllabus Area   Progress Theme

Syllabus Area	Question Number	Part	Marks
Progress Theme	7	A	6

	Using the Project Scenario, answer the following 6 questions about the use of PRINCE2 controls in this project.
1	At the end of initiation there is +1 week/-2 weeks' time tolerance for this project. Which statement is true?
	A There can be no time tolerances for any of the stages.
	B All of the project level time tolerance can be allocated to stage 2.
	C The Stage Plan for stage 2 could create some additional project time tolerance by allowing no time tolerance in Team Plans.
	D Additional time tolerance for the project could be found by adding extra resources without affecting other tolerances.
2	During stage 2, if the Project Manager decides to recommend that the Project Plan is revised to finish three weeks later, which statement is correct?
	A The tolerances stated in the Project Plan CANNOT be changed.
	B The Executive needs to seek formal approval from corporate management to implement this change.
	C Such a change might affect the Business Case, and therefore the current project would have to close prematurely and be restarted with a new Project Plan, a new Business Case and new Risk Register.
	D The revision of the Project Plan would have to wait until the end stage assessment of stage 2.
3	During stage 2, an early review of the photo design ideas from the Marketing department has highlighted the need for engineering machinery to be operating in the background during the photo sessions. This requires a change to the baselined Product Description for the photos. What action should the Project Manager take?
	A Log the change in the Issue Register as a request for change.
	B Raise an Exception Report to the Project Board.
	C Revise the Product Description for the photos and issue it to the Engineering Manager to ensure that the machinery will be operating during the photo sessions.
	D Include this requirement on the next Checkpoint Report to the photographer.

4	As the project approaches the end of stage 2, the Project Manager has requested a Product Status Account to ensure that all products are at their expected point of development. Although the list of customers has been quality reviewed, it has not been baselined because the Marketing department have not provided all of the prospective customers' details. What initial action should the Project Manager take?
	A Delay producing the End Stage Report until the list of customers has been baselined.
	B Raise an Exception Report to the Project Board to highlight the issue.
	C Check the target sign-off date for the list of customers.
	D Update the product status to baselined and obtain a commitment from the Marketing department to finish this work within the next few days.
5	Whilst identifying the mailing costs for the calendars the Project Manager was surprised to find the costs could vary considerably depending on the size of the package and the delivery service used. For the purpose of this project, the Project Manager has selected an appropriate service but feels that a corporate standard for postage would have reduced the time and effort invested. It could reduce the company's overheads by up to £20k per year. How should the Project Manager record this observation within the project?
	A Produce a project mandate, outlining the potential savings to be achieved by the introduction of a corporate standard.
	B Make a note of the observation in the Daily Log to be transferred to a Benefits Review Plan at the end of the project.
	C Record the observation in an Exception Report to the Project Board.
	D Make an entry in the Lessons Log for future consideration by corporate management.
6	The team member collating the list of customers has now forecast that it will NOT be complete by the end of this stage as originally planned, due to a number of new prospective customers' details not yet being available. What action should the team member take?
	A Report the forecast delay in the next Checkpoint Report to the Executive.
	B Add the product to the next Stage Plan in order to allocate additional resources and complete the work.
	C Make an entry in the Risk Register so the Project Manager can decide on appropriate action.
	D Raise an issue to inform the Project Manager.

Question Number 7 continued

Syllabus Area	Question Number	Part	Marks
Progress Theme	7	B	6

Using the Project Scenario, answer the following question.

Lines 1 to 6 in the table below consist of an assertion statement and a reason statement. For each line identify the appropriate option, from options A to E, that applies. Each option can be used once, more than once or not at all.

Option	Assertion	Reason	
A	True	True	AND the reason explains the assertion
B	True	True	BUT the reason does not explain the assertion
C	True	False	
D	False	True	
E	False	False	

	Assertion		Reason
1	The label design competition should be planned and managed as two management stages.	BECAUSE	A decision can only be made by the Project Board at the end of a management stage.
2	Quality tolerances allocated to the photos can be used to remedy a forecast threat to time tolerance.	BECAUSE	Any forecast threat to time tolerance should first be resolved by use of any available quality tolerance.
3	A suitable point for a stage boundary would be after the production cost forecast has been produced.	BECAUSE	A stage boundary represents a go/no go decision point.
4	With +1 week / -2 weeks time tolerance, the project is permitted to finish two weeks later than 30 November.	BECAUSE	A negative project time tolerance indicates the total permissible delay to a project schedule before an exception situation occurs.
5	If the project is forecast to exceed the cost tolerance of +£6k, the Project Manager should send an Exception Report straight to corporate management.	BECAUSE	If the forecast is for project tolerances to be exceeded, the Project Board no longer has the authority to continue with the project.
6	The production cost forecast should be reviewed by the Project Board during the Directing a Project process to determine whether the project should continue.	BECAUSE	The Project Board reviews all products at the end of each stage.

QUESTION NUMBER 8
Syllabus Area   Change Theme

Syllabus Area	Question Number	Part	Marks
Change Theme	8	A	6

Using the Project Scenario answer the following question. The Plan for stage 3 has been approved and work has commenced.

Column 1 contains a number of issues for this project. Select from Column 2 the appropriate category for each issue. Each selection from Column 2 can be used once, more than once or not at all.

	Column 1	Column 2
1	Although NOT previously considered, the Engineering Manager now wants to amend the Product Description for the photos to include images of his latest production machinery.	A Problem or concern B Request for change C Off-specification
2	The Marketing Director feels that the calendar may NOT be of sufficient quality to achieve the projected benefits.	
3	The Marketing department have identified some new customers and want to include them in the approved list of customers.	
4	The photographer has ignored the agreed photo session schedule. He has interrupted the work of the engineering staff to take the photos for the calendar.	
5	The chosen label design has been signed-off in error as the old company logo has been used. Inclusion of the new company logo was specified.	
6	The Project Manager has received notification of a postal strike occurring in December.	

Question Number 8 continued

Syllabus Area	Question Number	Part	Marks
Change Theme	8	B	6

There is a major concern over an apparent lack of control of project documentation.

For each concern listed in Column 1, select from Column 2 the configuration management task that could help address the problem. Each selection from Column 2 can be used once, more than once or not at all.

	Column 1	Column 2
1	As a number of people are involved in the project it is becoming increasingly difficult to keep track of what documentation each person has.	A Produce a Product Status Account B Maintain a record of all copies issued C Record the link between version and the Issue Report that caused its change D Notify copy holders of any changes E Recall and archive superseded product copies F Retain master products, issuing copies only G Maintain a record of relationships between products
2	Both current and previous versions of the photo session are in circulation.	
3	A revised list of customers has been issued but it is not clear what was wrong with the previous one.	
4	The Marketing department has lost the chosen label design and no copy was made.	
5	The Marketing department staff cannot say with any certainty which photos were approved and which still require work.	
6	The Engineering Manager has complained that the photo session schedule has been changed and that no consideration has been given to the impact this will have on the engineering staff shift pattern.	

QUESTION NUMBER 9

Syllabus Area   Directing a Project + Managing a Stage Boundary + Closing a Project Processes

Syllabus Area	Question Number	Part	Marks
Directing a Project + Managing a Stage Boundary + Closing a Project Processes	9	A	6

Using the Project Scenario, answer the following 6 questions.

It is now late October and the project is in stage 3. The label design competition has been held and the photos of the staff have been taken. The CEO and Marketing Director still need to choose the winning label design and the 12 photos for the calendar. However, the Executive has learned that two competitors are issuing calendars to MNO's customers by the middle of November. After analysing the impact of this issue, one of the options the Project Manager has presented to the Project Board is to close the project prematurely.

There are a number of key facts relating to this project that would need to be recorded if the project were to be closed now.

1	Which product should show that the photos could be used for other promotional material for the company?
	A Benefits Review Plan
	B Lessons Log
	C Exception Report
	D End Project Report
2	Which product should show that the staff photo sessions were disruptive to the Engineering Department as they had been scheduled during peak work times without consultation with the Engineering Manager?
	A Follow-on action recommendations
	B Lessons Report
	C Project closure notification
	D Risk Register
3	Which product should show that if anybody has any remaining resource costs to be charged to the project, they should ensure this is done by 10 November?
	A Benefits Review Plan
	B End Project Report
	C Follow-on action recommendations
	D Project closure notification

Question Number 9 continued

4	Which product should show that the project has been closed prematurely and has not achieved the objectives defined in the Project Initiation Documentation (PID)?
	A Benefits Review Plan
	B End Project Report
	C Exception Report
	D Project closure notification
5	Which product should show that without the calendar the company is going to experience difficulties recovering its decline in orders, and alternative solutions are required if the company is going to recover its position?
	A Benefits Review Plan
	B Exception Report
	C End Project Report
	D Risk Register
6	Which product should register that the risk of a competitor producing a calendar at the same time was identified at the beginning of the project but the assessment of this risk appears to have been poor?
	A Issue Register
	B Follow-on action recommendations
	C Lessons Report
	D Risk Register

Syllabus Area	Question Number	Part	Marks
Directing a Project + Managing a Stage Boundary + Closing a Project Processes	9	B	6

Using the Project Scenario, answer the following question.

The Calendar project was delivered as originally planned, and is now preparing for planned closure.

Lines 1 to 6 in the table below consist of an assertion statement and a reason statement. For each line identify the appropriate option, from options A to E, that applies. Each option can be used once, more than once or not at all.

Option	Assertion	Reason	
A	True	True	AND the reason explains the assertion
B	True	True	BUT the reason does not explain the assertion
C	True	False	
D	False	True	
E	False	False	

	Assertion		Reason
1	Whether the calendar achieves its objective of countering the decline in orders will be confirmed in the Closing a Project process.	BECAUSE	The Benefits Review Plan is created in the Closing a Project process.
2	A formal quality review meeting, chaired by the Project Manager, should be held for the Project Board to compare the final deliverable against the Project Product Description.	BECAUSE	The Project Product Description is used by the Closing a Project process to verify that the project has delivered what was expected of it.
3	The End Project Report must be completed before 30 November.	BECAUSE	An End Project Report should be produced before a project closes.
4	The Stage Plan for stage 3 should contain details of the products to be created or updated during the Closing a Project process.	BECAUSE	Closure activities should be planned as part of the Stage Plan for the final management stage.

Question Number 9 continued

5	As part of the handover of the final product a contract should be agreed with Marketing for ongoing support of this product.	BECAUSE	A service agreement or maintenance contract should always be included as a product of the final stage.
6	At the end of stage 3, the Managing a Stage Boundary process should be used to update the Project Plan with actuals from the final stage.	BECAUSE	An objective of the Managing a Stage Boundary process is to review, and if necessary, update the Project Initiation Documentation.

The Practitioner Examination

MARKING SCHEME

Exam Paper: GB-EX02-1.6

Booklet is view only. No answer data has been created.

Question	Part	Type	Response	A	B	C	D	E	F	G	H	I
1	A	MR	1	0	1	0	0	1				
			2	1	0	0	0	1				
			3	1	0	1	0	0				
			4	0	1	0	1	0				
			5	0	0	1	1	0				
			6	0	1	0	0	1				
			7	0	0	1	1	0				
	B	AR	1	0	0	1	0	0				
			2	0	0	0	0	1				
			3	1	0	0	0	0				
			4	0	1	0	0	0				
			5	0	0	0	0	1				

Question	Part	Type	Response	A	B	C	D	E	F	G	H	I
2	A	MR	1	0	0	1	1	0				
			2	0	0	0	1	1				
			3	1	0	1	0	0				
			4	0	0	1	0	1				
			5	1	1	0	0	0				
			6	0	1	1	0	0				
			7	1	0	0	0	1				
	B	AR	1	0	0	0	1	0				
			2	0	0	0	0	1				
			3	0	0	0	0	1				
			4	1	0	0	0	0				
			5	0	1	0	0	0				

Question	Part	Type	Response	A	B	C	D	E	F	G	H	I
3	A	MG	1	0	0	1						
			2	0	1	0						
			3	1	0	0						
	B	MG	1	0	1	0	0	0				
			2	1	0	0	0	0				
			3	0	0	0	0	1				
			4	0	0	1	0	0				
	C	MR	1	1	1	0	0	0				
			2	0	0	1	1	0				
			3	0	0	0	1	1				
			4	0	1	0	0	1				
			5	1	0	1	0	0				

Question	Part	Type	Response	A	B	C	D	E	F	G	H	I
4	A	CL	1	0	1	0						
			2	0	0	1						
			3	1	0	0						
			4	0	0	1						
			5	1	0	0						
	B	CL	1	0	0	1						
			2	0	1	0						
			3	0	1	0						
			4	1	0	0						
			5	0	1	0						
			6	1	0	0						
			7	0	0	1						

Question	Part	Type	Response	A	B	C	D	E	F	G	H	I
5	A	MG	1	0	0	0	0	1	0			
			2	1	0	0	0	0	0			
			3	0	1	0	0	0	0			
			4	0	0	1	0	0	0			
			5	0	0	0	0	1	0			
			6	0	1	0	0	0	0			
	B	AR	1	0	1	0	0	0				
			2	1	0	0	0	0				
			3	0	0	1	0	0				
			4	0	0	0	0	1				
			5	1	0	0	0	0				
			6	0	0	0	0	1				

Question	Part	Type	Response	A	B	C	D	E	F	G	H	I
6	A	MG	1	0	1	0	0					
			2	1	0	0	0					
			3	1	0	0	0					
			4	0	0	0	1					
			5	0	0	0	1					
			6	0	0	0	1					
			7	0	0	1	0					
	B	MR	1	1	0	1	0	0				
			2	0	0	0	1	1				
			3	1	0	0	0	1				
			4	1	1	0	0	0				
			5	1	0	0	1	0				

Question	Part	Type	Response	A	B	C	D	E	F	G	H	I
7	A	CL	1	0	1	0	0					
			2	0	1	0	0					
			3	1	0	0	0					
			4	0	0	1	0					
			5	0	0	0	1					
			6	0	0	0	1					
	B	AR	1	0	0	0	0	1				
			2	0	0	1	0	0				
			3	1	0	0	0	0				
			4	0	0	0	0	1				
			5	0	0	0	1	0				
			6	0	0	1	0	0				

Question	Part	Type	Response	A	B	C	D	E	F	G	H	I
8	A	MG	1	0	1	0						
			2	1	0	0						
			3	0	1	0						
			4	1	0	0						
			5	0	0	1						
			6	1	0	0						
	B	MG	1	0	1	0	0	0	0	0		
			2	0	0	0	0	1	0	0		
			3	0	0	1	0	0	0	0		
			4	0	0	0	0	0	1	0		
			5	1	0	0	0	0	0	0		
			6	0	0	0	0	0	0	1		

Question	Part	Type	Response	A	B	C	D	E	F	G	H	I
9	A	CL	1	0	0	0	1					
			2	0	1	0	0					
			3	0	0	0	1					
			4	0	1	0	0					
			5	0	0	1	0					
			6	0	0	1	0					
	B	AR	1	0	0	0	0	1				
			2	0	0	0	1	0				
			3	0	0	0	1	0				
			4	1	0	0	0	0				
			5	0	0	0	0	1				
			6	0	0	0	1	0				

The Practitioner Examination

RATIONALE

Exam Paper: GB-EX02-1.6

Question: 1, Part: A, Type: MR			
1	A	Incorrect:	This is an Expected Benefit of this project. The Reasons should show why the project outcome is needed, the background.
	B	Correct:	This is an explanation of why the project is required.
	C	Incorrect:	This is the total number of orders last year, the position to measure against. It is not the expected benefit for this project.
	D	Incorrect:	This is an Expected Benefit of this project. The Reasons should show why the project outcome is needed, the background.
	E	Correct:	This is an explanation of why the project is required.
2	A	Correct:	This is one of the options considered to achieve the project outcome.
	B	Incorrect:	Thus is an approach to deliver the required products and should therefore be documented in the Project Brief.
	C	Incorrect:	This is an approach to deliver the required products and should therefore be documented in the Project Brief.
	D	Incorrect:	This is an approach to deliver the required products and should therefore be documented in the Project Brief.
	E	Correct:	This option is always considered in the Business Case as a starting point to act as a comparison for other options.

3	A	Correct:	This is a stated measurable benefit anticipated from this project.
	B	Incorrect:	Using a similar format to previous years may have contributed to the selection of the business option but it is not a project benefit.
	C	Correct:	This is a stated measurable benefit anticipated from this project.
	D	Incorrect:	The Business Case does not contain a breakdown of the products to be delivered within the project.
	E	Incorrect:	This is a requirement of the project product which should be stated in the Project Product Description.
4	A	Incorrect:	This relates to the cost of quality within the deliverables. It is NOT a negative consequence of the project.
	B	Correct:	This is a negative consequence of the calendar project.
	C	Incorrect:	This is a threat to the expected benefits, NOT a negative consequence of the project.
	D	Correct:	This is negative consequence of the calendar project.
	E	Incorrect:	This is a threat to the expected benefits, NOT a negative consequence of the project.
5	A	Incorrect:	This is a risk. It has not happened yet, but the impact should be considered and recorded under 'Major Risks'.
	B	Incorrect:	The recruitment campaign is likely to be a follow-on action that is not within the scope of this project.
	C	Correct:	When benefits are expected to be achieved should be stated under the Timescale heading in the Business Case.
	D	Correct:	This is the timescale for project delivery and should be stated here under the heading of Timescale.
	E	Incorrect:	This is not a timescale for project delivery.
6	A	Incorrect:	The fact that MNO have allocated £120k to the marketing budget for this year is not a cost of the project.
	B	Correct:	The Business Case should show the funding arrangements under the heading of Costs within the Business Case.
	C	Incorrect:	This is an Expected Benefit, it is not a cost of the project, i.e. expected income rather than outgoings.
	D	Incorrect:	The new company logo is not within the scope of this project.
	E	Correct:	The costs section of the Business Case should include the total of forecast costs, including allocated tolerances, risk and change budgets.

7	A	Incorrect:	This is a dis-benefit of the project outcome, not a risk to the project.
	B	Incorrect:	This is not a risk, this is stated as fact in the Project Scenario.
	C	Correct:	This is a risk to the project. Risks facing the project can either reduce/enhance the benefits or reduce/increase the cost.
	D	Correct:	This is a risk to the project. Risks facing the project can either reduce/enhance the benefits or reduce/increase the cost.
	E	Incorrect:	This does not describe a correctly defined risk and provide a clear and unambiguous expression of the cause, event and effect. Ref 8.3.5.1

Question: 1, Part: B, Type: AR				
1	True:	The costs of the project may impact the project viability and the Business Case must reflect this.	False:	Options considered for the delivery of the chosen solution should be covered in the project approach (Project Brief). Ref A.19.2. The business options in the Business Case refer to the various solutions considered. Ref A.2.2.
2	False:	Printing within the first week of December remains within the project's time tolerance of +1 week.	False:	Further tolerance may be available for the stage in which case the Business Case may still be viable.
3	True:	The outline Business Case contains the reasons why the project is needed and forms part of the Project Brief.	True:	The Project Brief includes high-level information on what needs to be done, why, who will need to be involved, and how and when it will be done. Ref A.19.2. This reason explains the assertion, therefore the answer is A.
4	True:	The Benefits Review Plan is used to define for the Executive how and when a measurement of the achievements of the project's benefits can be made.	True:	At the end of each stage the Benefits Review Plan will be examined and reviewed for the results of any benefits reviews undertaken during the stage. Ref 17.4.3. The assertion refers to some time after the project has closed. Therefore the answer is B.
5	False:	This is a positive consequence of the Calendar project which is measurable and should therefore be recorded in the Business Case.	False:	All benefits, both financial and non-financial, should be recorded in the Business Case. Ref A.2.2.

Question: 2, Part: A, Type: MR			
1	A	Incorrect:	The length of service of an individual is not a PRINCE2 reason for the appointment of an Executive. Ref 5.3.2.2.
	B	Incorrect:	Although this may be useful from a specialist knowledge point of view, this is not a PRINCE2 reason for the appointment of an Executive. Ref 5.3.2.2.
	C	Correct:	An Executive should be able to represent the business interests on a project. Ref 5.3.2.2.
	D	Correct:	The Executive should be able to commit resources to the project and make decisions on behalf of the business. Ref 5.3.2.2.
	E	Incorrect:	The development needs of an individual are not a PRINCE2 reason for the appointment of an Executive. Ref 5.3.2.2.
2	A	Incorrect:	The length of service of an individual is not a PRINCE2 reason for the appointment of an Executive. Ref 5.3.2.2.
	B	Incorrect:	Knowledge of a functional position is not a PRINCE2 reason for the appointment of an Executive. Ref 5.3.2.2.
	C	Incorrect:	Physical involvement is not a PRINCE2 reason for the appointment of an Executive. Ref 5.3.2.2.
	D	Correct:	The Executive should be able to commit resources and make decisions on behalf of the business. Ref 5.3.2.2.
	E	Correct:	The Executive has knowledge of the business strategic requirements and a responsibility to ensure that the project is aligned to these strategies. Ref 5.3.2.2.
3	A	Correct:	The Senior User should be able to make decisions on behalf of the users and as a representative of the main users of the deliverable from the project the Marketing Director would be suitable for this role. Ref 5.3.2.2.
	B	Incorrect:	This would be useful for the role responsible for supplying the specialist knowledge for this project. The Senior User role does not require specialist knowledge. Ref 5.3.2.2.
	C	Correct:	The Senior User should represent those for whom the product will achieve an objective or those who will use the products to deliver benefits. Ref 5.3.2.2.
	D	Incorrect:	The Executive role represents the funding of the project, not the Senior User. Ref 5.3.2.2.
	E	Incorrect:	Those producing the products within the project are suppliers and should be represented by the Senior Supplier. Ref 5.3.2.2.

4	A	Incorrect:	The length of service and motivation of an individual is not a PRINCE2 reason for the appointment of a Senior User. Ref 5.3.2.2.
	B	Incorrect:	The development needs of an individual are not a PRINCE2 reason for the appointment of a Senior User. Ref 5.3.2.2.
	C	Correct:	The Senior User should represent those who are affected by the project. Ref 5.3.2.2.
	D	Incorrect:	PRINCE2 does not recognise reporting structures within the business or hierarchies. The reporting structure within the project will be agreed within the project. Ref 5.3.2.2.
	E	Correct:	The Senior User should represent the interests of those who will use the final product(s) of the project. Ref 5.3.2.2.
5	A	Correct:	The project may need a temporary appointment for the Senior Supplier role – perhaps from the customer's procurement department. The Senior Supplier represents the interests of those procuring the project's products. Ref 5.3.2.2.
	B	Correct:	PRINCE2 suggests that one option for the Senior Supplier role is to appoint the person who is responsible for the performance of the supplier contract. Ref 5.3.2.2.
	C	Incorrect:	The Purchasing Manager's experience of Engineering has no bearing on the project or the role of Senior Supplier within the project. Ref 5.3.2.2.
	D	Incorrect:	It is highly unlikely that an external supplier would let a customer organization influence their Business Case. Ref 5.3.2.2.
	E	Incorrect:	Just because an individual is not appropriate for the role of Executive or Senior User, does not make them appropriate as a Senior Supplier Ref 5.3.2.2.
6	A	Incorrect:	The length of service and motivation of an individual is not a PRINCE2 reason for the appointment of a Project Assurance role. Ref 5.3.2.2.
	B	Correct:	As a user of the project's product(s), the Sales Manager would be well placed to evaluate the impact of potential changes from the user point of view on behalf of the Senior User, which is a Project Assurance responsibility. Ref 5.3.2.2.
	C	Correct:	Current and prospective customers are stakeholders within the project and the Sales Manager is well placed to advise on how best to communicate with them, a role of the User Assurance. Ref 5.3.2.2.
	D	Incorrect:	The development needs of an individual are not a PRINCE2 reason for the appointment of a Project Assurance role. Ref 5.3.2.2.
	E	Incorrect:	The resolution of conflicts between users is a responsibility of the Senior User, not Project Assurance. Ref 5.3.2.2.

7	A	Correct:	Unless appointed to another person, Project Support perform the configuration management procedure. Ref 5.3.2.8.
	B	Incorrect:	The length of service and general existence is not a PRINCE2 reason for the appointment of a Project Support role. Ref 5.3.2.8.
	C	Incorrect:	This is a quality assurance responsibility which may be delegated to Project Assurance, but NOT Project Support. Ref 6.2.6.
	D	Incorrect:	The quality assurance function may be delegated to Project Assurance, but NOT Project Support. Ref 6.2.6.
	E	Correct:	This is a competency required of Project Support. Ref 5.3.2.8.

Question: 2, Part: B, Type: AR

1	False:	The Executive role is vested in one individual so that there is a single point of accountability for the project. Ref 5.3.2.2.	True:	The Executive is ultimately responsible for the project and would seek approval for the investment from corporate or programme management. Ref C2.1.
2	False:	The Senior User role can be shared by more than one individual (Ref 5.3.2.2) but the Engineering Manager does not represent a user on this project.	False:	The Senior User commits user resources for the purpose of quality checking. It is the Senior Supplier role that provides specialist resources for the design and development of the project's products. Ref 5.3.2.2.
3	False:	More than one supplier may perform a Senior Supplier role on a project, making decisions and committing resources on behalf of their organizations. Ref 5.3.2.2.	False:	The Senior Supplier role can be performed by internal and/or external resources, depending on what is being supplied during the project. Ref 5.3.2.2.
4	True:	Project Support and Project Assurance roles should be kept separate in order to maintain the independence of Project Assurance. Ref 5.3.2.8.	True:	Project Assurance must be kept separate to Project Support in order to maintain their independence. Ref 5.3.2.8. This is an explanation of the assertion, therefore the answer is A.
5	True:	The Engineering Manager is a stakeholder from within the organization, but external to the project management team. He is not a supplier or a user, but he does have an interest and some influence. Ref 5.3.5.3.	True:	The Communication Management Strategy describes the tools to be used for each step in the communication process. Ref A.4.2. This is not why the Engineering Manager should be included, therefore the answer is B.

Question: 3, Part: A, Type: MG		
1	Correct [C]:	Quality Planning – This covers agreement on overall quality expectations, the products required with their associated quality criteria, the means by which quality will be achieved and assessed. Ref 6.3.1.
2	Correct [B]:	Quality Control – This covers the activities undertaken by the project team to ensure that the products meet their respective quality criteria. Ref 6.3.2.
3	Correct [A]:	Quality Assurance – This activity manages the organization's Quality Management System, not part of the project. Ref 6.2.6.

Question: 3, Part: B, Type: MG		
1	Correct [B]:	This states a measurable requirement of the product and should be noted under Quality Criteria. Ref A17.2
2	Correct [A]:	This is not measurable as a quality criteria, it provides no details of what would be an acceptable deviation from this (tolerance) and does not refer to any skills of people required. It is therefore not included. Ref A17.2.
3	Correct [E]:	The Project Board will be asked to review the label entries and will therefore appear as reviewer under quality responsibilities. Ref A17.2.
4	Correct [C]:	Given the quality criteria, this is a measure of what would be acceptable as a quality tolerance. Ref A17.2.

Question: 3, Part: C, Type: MR			
1	A	Correct:	The product is selected paper, and not the paper itself. Ref A.21.2.
	B	Correct:	This is not a major product to be delivered by this project. Ref A.21.2.
	C	Incorrect:	This is a major product to be delivered by this project, derived from Marketing and Accounts information. Ref A.21.2.
	D	Incorrect:	Regardless of the source, this is a major product to be delivered by the project. Ref A.21.2.
	E	Incorrect:	This is beyond the scope of this project. The final product will be the prepared calendar pack. Ref A.21.2

2	A	Incorrect:	The new logo design is being created by another project and therefore is not within scope. Ref A.21.2
	B	Incorrect:	This already exists and it provides the basis upon which this calendar will be designed. The design of the calendar will incorporate the design of the new logo. It is therefore a derivation and should not be moved. Ref A.21.2.
	C	Correct:	The Internal Creative team will be required to create products and are therefore already correctly shown under Development skills required. Ref A.21.2
	D	Correct:	This is a product to be delivered by this project. Ref A.21.2.
	E	Incorrect:	This is not a source product from which the project is derived. Ref A.21.2.
3	A	Incorrect:	This is a supplier to this project, it is not a major product to be delivered by this project. Ref A.21.2.
	B	Incorrect:	This is a supplier to this project, it is not a derivation or source of information for this project. Ref A.21.2.
	C	Incorrect:	Project management is a skill or process. It is not a major product to be delivered by this project. Ref A.21.2.
	D	Correct:	The printing of the calendar is outside of the scope of this project. Ref A.21.2.
	E	Correct:	This skill/person/group is required to help create the customer list. Ref A.21.2.
4	A	Incorrect:	This is one of the quality expectations stated, the photos are to be professional. Ref A.21.2.
	B	Correct:	Printing is beyond the scope of this project. Ref A.21.2.
	C	Incorrect:	Customer's quality expectations are a description of the quality expected of the Project Product and the standards and processes that will need to be applied to achieve that quality. Ref A.21.2.
	D	Incorrect:	This is stated as a customer quality expectation, a description of the quality expected of the Project Product and the standards and processes that will need to be applied to achieve that quality. Ref A.21.2.
	E	Correct:	This is an expected benefit (positive consequence) of this project and should not be recorded under customer's quality expectations. Ref A.21.2.

5	A	Correct:	The existing entry is not measurable, attractive and humorous are not defined. This is a measurable definition of the attributes that must apply to the set of products to be acceptable to key stakeholders. Ref A.21.2.
	B	Incorrect:	Acceptance criteria can be expressed as many things, including appearance. This is not a composition item. Ref A.21.2.
	C	Correct:	The new company logo is being produced by another project. It is required for inclusion within the Calendar project but the quality of it will not be assessed during this project. Ref A.21.2.
	D	Incorrect:	This is a measurable definition of the criteria that the Project Product must meet before the customer will accept. Derivation provides the source from which the product will be created. Ref A21.2.
	E	Incorrect:	Acceptance criteria can be expressed as many things including accuracy so long as it is measurable. Dates are to be shown correctly as stated in the Scenario. Ref A.21.2.

Question: 4, Part: A, Type: CL			
1	A	Incorrect:	Plans can be presented in many ways. The use of a graphical timeline or schedule is not mandatory. Ref 19.5.1.1.
	B	Correct:	A simple plan in the form of a schedule of who is involved in producing, reviewing and approving products together with key milestones. This is often referred to as a product checklist. Ref 19.5.1.1.
	C	Incorrect:	Team Plans are detailed and of different durations. These will not provide the Project Board with an overall baseline for tracking the project's progress. Ref 7.2.4 and 19.5.1.1.
2	A	Incorrect:	The Quality Management Strategy does not contain this information. Ref A22.
	B	Incorrect:	In simple projects it is acceptable for the PID to be created directly from the project mandate. Ref 19.5.1.2.
	C	Correct:	The Project Product Description is approved as part of the PID and should contain the customer's quality expectations. Ref 19.5.1.3 / A21.
3	A	Correct:	Each stage should have a Stage Plan and the use of two further stages provides the appropriate controlled break for the Project Board to decide whether to continue or not. Ref 10.3.2.
	B	Incorrect:	Whilst the number of stages in a project is flexible, the use of PRINCE2 stages is mandated. There must be at least the Initiation Stage and a delivery stage. The activities would be in the Project Plan not the Initiation Stage Plan. Ref 10.3.2/19.5.1.3.
	C	Incorrect:	The activities of the Closing a Project process should be scheduled as part of the final stage, not a stage in its own right. Ref 18.3.

4	A	Incorrect:	The Benefits Review Plan is updated at the end of each stage, but the original plan forms part of the justification for the project and should be created (in some form) during the initiation stage. Ref 14.4.7.
	B	Incorrect:	The Benefits Review Plan is created in Initiating a Project and updated toward the end of each stage with actual benefits achieved and a revised plan for any remaining benefit reviews whether within or beyond the life of the project. Ref 14.4.7.
	C	Correct:	In a small/simple project it is acceptable to have the Benefits Review Plan, the Project Product Description and Product Descriptions as part of the Project Plan. Ref 19.5.1.3.
5	A	Correct:	The Daily Log can be used to record this information during Starting up a Project before the Issue and Risk Registers are created during initiation. In a simple project, the Daily Log could continue to be used throughout the project for this purpose. Ref 19.5.1.3.
	B	Incorrect:	Separate registers are not mandated. The Daily Log can be used to record this information during Starting up a Project before the Issue and Risk Registers are created in initiation, or the Daily Log could continue to be used for this purpose. Ref.19.5.1.3.
	C	Incorrect:	Separate registers are not mandated. In a simple project, the Daily Log can be used to record issues, risks and lessons throughout the project. Ref 19.5.1.3. But this is a separate document not held within the PID.

Question: 4, Part: B, Type: CL			
1	A	Incorrect:	The focus should be on communication to/from those internal and external to the project, not only the project management team. These may be external to the company not just within MNO. Ref A4.
	B	Incorrect:	The focus should not be on control and reporting. The focus should be on communication to/from parties both internal and external to the project. Ref A4.
	C	Correct:	Facilitates the engagement with stakeholders through the establishment of a controlled flow of information. Ref A4.
2	A	Incorrect:	This only provides for internal communications. Processes need also to include external communications. Ref A4.
	B	Correct:	External interested parties (to the project) may be internal and/or external to the organization. Process section needs to provide for communications both internal and external to the project. Ref A4.
	C	Incorrect:	Reference to standard communication methods rather than reciting the standard is acceptable. Any variance from corporate or programme management standards should be highlighted, together with the justification for the variance. Ref A4.

3	A	Incorrect:	The staff newsletter is a tool for communicating to a stakeholder group within this project. Ref A4.
	B	Correct:	The reporting section describes any reports that are to be produced on the communication process, their purpose, timing and recipients (for example, performance indicators). Ref A4.
	C	Incorrect:	The company website is a tool for communicating to the customers, a project stakeholder group. Ref A4.
4	A	Correct:	Details about the information held for each of the project's products is documented in the Configuration Management Strategy, not the Communication Management Strategy. Ref A6.
	B	Incorrect:	The records section of the Communication Management strategy should show what communication records will be required and where they will be stored. Ref A4.
	C	Incorrect:	The records section of the Communication Management Strategy should show what communication records will be required and where they will be stored. Ref A4.
5	A	Incorrect:	Performance audits of the communication procedure are recommended as part of the communication activities. This is a valid entry for this heading. Ref A4.
	B	Correct:	The timing of communication activities section states when formal communication activities are to be undertaken (i.e. at the end of a stage) including performance audits of the communication methods. Ref A4.
	C	Incorrect:	Highlight Reports are also a method of communicating to external stakeholders. This should not be removed. Ref A4.
6	A	Correct:	The Internal Creative Team are stakeholders within this project. Their information needs will need to be considered and planned for. Ref A4.
	B	Incorrect:	The Information Needs section contains a description of the means and frequency of communication to parties both internal and external to the project. Ref A4.
	C	Incorrect:	Whilst the printing of the calendars is not within the scope of the project, the print company are an interested party and will need to be kept informed of the designs and progress, etc. Ref A4.
7	A	Incorrect:	This shows the method and frequency with which the project will provide information to the stakeholder producing the staff newsletter. Ref A4.
	B	Incorrect:	The Information Needs section should show the method and frequency with which the project will provide information to the stakeholder producing the staff newsletter. Ref A4.
	C	Correct:	This relates to the development of a product and those people who are required to provide information or those who need to receive information in order to complete an acceptable product. Ref A4.

Question: 5, Part: A, Type: MG		
1	Correct [E]:	'Accept' – A conscious decision to do nothing but monitor and ensure that the threat remains tolerable. Ref Table 8.2.
2	Correct [A]:	'Avoid' – By not completing the project, changing some aspect of the project so that the threat can no longer have an impact or can no longer happen. Ref Table 8.2.
3	Correct [B]:	'Reduce' – Bringing the delivery date forward is a form of proactive action taken to reduce the probability and/or the impact of the event should it occur. Ref Table 8.2.
4	Correct [C]:	'Fallback' – Waiting to see if a rival calendar is produced and developing a plan for extra incentives to be implemented after the risk occurs will reduce the impact, but not the probability. Ref Table 8.2.
5	Correct [E]:	'Accept' – A conscious decision to do nothing but monitor and ensure that the threat remains tolerable. Ref Table 8.2.
6	Correct [B]:	'Reduce' – This does not stop the risk from occurring but is a form of proactive action taken to reduce the probability and/or the impact of the event should it occur. Ref Table 8.2.

Question: 5, Part: B, Type: AR				
1	True:	This could have an effect on the project and should therefore be brought to the attention of the Project Manager as an issue (problem). Ref 9.2.4.	True:	At stage level, exception situations should be escalated to the Project Board in an Exception Report. This does not explain the assertion, the answer is therefore B. Ref 10.3.4.
2	True:	The Purchasing Manager should be monitoring the contract situation and is therefore the person best situated to keep an eye on this risk. Ref 8.3.5.4.	True:	The risk owner is responsible for managing the actions taken to manage the risk. These actions may be delegated to a Risk Actionee, but the Risk Owner remains responsible. This reason explains the assertion, the answer is therefore A. Ref 8.3.5.4.
3	True:	When accepting a Work Package a Team Manager should perform a risk analysis identifying any risks, and the means of managing them. Ref 16.4.1.	False:	There is only one Risk Register for the project, created during Initiating a Project. Ref 14.4.1.
4	False:	If a risk is likely to impact upon time, the proposed risk response should mitigate this. Only when the risk occurs, does it become an Issue Report. Ref 8.3.5.	False:	Risk action may be implemented within tolerance or risk budget if there is one. An Issue Report would be required if the cost of the risk action were to exceed tolerance. Ref 8.3.5.

| 5 | True: | The Checkpoint Report is a major data gathering tool for the Project Manager and should contain a summary of the risk status. Ref 8.3.5.5/ 16.4.1. | True: | The Checkpoint Report will provide a summary of actual and forecast progress, highlighting any potential areas for concern. This explains the assertion, the answer is therefore A. Ref A.3. |
| 6 | False: | This is not an acceptable risk response. Although the Project Manager may decide to manage by exception they are still responsible for risk management. Ref Table 8.2. | False: | When selecting the risk response, it is a question of balancing the cost of taking that response against the likelihood and impact of allowing the risk to occur. Ref 8.3.5.3. |

Question: 6, Part: A, Type: MG	
1	Correct [B]:	The production cost forecast is a product being produced within the scope of this project. It should therefore NOT appear in an ellipse. This is an internal product incorrectly shown as an external product. Ref 7.3.3.2.
2	Correct [A]:	The tariff of mailing costs is being supplied by the Post Office and already exists. This is therefore an external product not shown correctly (should be shown in an ellipse in this instance). Ref 7.3.3.2.
3	Correct [A]:	The photo design ideas are being supplied by Marketing and already exist. They are therefore an external product not shown correctly (should be shown in an ellipse in this instance). Ref 7.3.3.2.
4	Correct [D]:	The accounts information already exists and will form part of the list of customers. This is therefore correctly shown as an external product. Ref 7.3.3.2.
5	Correct [D]:	The monthly calendar displays are within the scope of this project. They are part of the calendar group and are not broken down further. They are therefore correctly shown as a product. Ref 7.3.3.2.
6	Correct [D]:	The label design is within the scope of this project. Ref 7.3.3.2.
7	Correct [C]:	Select photos is an activity and is therefore not a product. The product would be the selected photos. Ref 7.3.3.

Question: 6, Part: B, Type: MR			
1	A	Correct:	Whilst the Project Board would, in Directing a Project, assess whether the planned benefits could still be achieved, the actual benefits themselves are clearly not a prerequisite for the stage. Ref A16.2.
	B	Incorrect:	Whilst this is a deliverable of stage 2, the Project Board must agree to this in their decision to progress to stage 3. It is a major product of this project and the reason for the stage boundary. It is a pre-requisite of stage 3. Ref A16.2.
	C	Correct:	This is not a plan prerequisite for stage 3. As a product of stage 2 this should have been quality checked and signed-off , but work can commence on stage 3 even if this product is incomplete. Ref A16.2.
	D	Incorrect:	This is not a prerequisite of the stage. The stage can commence without the engineering staff, but may be delayed if they are not available when required. This may be identified as a risk. Ref A16.2.
	E	Incorrect:	This is confirmed during stage 2. The results of this check are not a prerequisite for stage 3. Work can commence without this. Ref A16.2.
2	A	Incorrect:	This is a deliverable that is not created within the scope of this project, but may influence the plan, it is therefore an external dependency. Ref A16.2.
	B	Incorrect:	This is not required for stage 3 to start. This is a deliverable that is not created within the scope of this project, but may influence the plan. Ref A16.2.
	C	Incorrect:	The logo is required during stage 3, but is not created within the scope of this project. Ref A16.2.
	D	Correct:	This is within the scope of this project and as a product of stage 2 this should have been quality checked and signed-off. Ref 16.4.2 / A16.2.
	E	Correct:	Whilst the company logo is an external dependency, the composition of the label design should be shown in the relevant Product Description. Ref A17.2
3	A	Correct:	The label designs are to be delivered during this stage, however, the results of the competition are unknown and cannot be qualified. This is therefore an assumption. Ref A16.2.
	B	Incorrect:	The label designs are within the scope of this project. If external resources are required to create a product, the product does not then become external, it is still within the scope of this project. Ref 7.3.3.2.
	C	Incorrect:	The operational staff schedule on which the photo session is based is updated weekly. The availability of staff shown in the photo session schedule may now be incorrect. Ref A16.2.
	D	Incorrect:	This product is produced by an external resource, within the scope of this project. It is not an external dependency. Ref 7.3.3.2.
	E	Correct:	Whilst this is a requirement, the composition of the photos should be shown in the relevant Product Description. Ref A16.2.

4	A	Correct:	It is the Stage Plan that is updated with actuals throughout the stage. Ref 15.4.4. The Project Plan is updated at the end of each stage. Ref 17.4.2.
	B	Correct:	This is an information need for corporate management recorded in the wrong document, the Project Board, not corporate management, would have responsibility for monitoring the stage. Ref A4.
	C	Incorrect:	The Highlight Report is a management product. The Product Descriptions section shows the specialist products of the plan. Ref A16.2.
	D	Incorrect:	The frequency at which the stage will be reviewed should be recorded here. Ref A16.2.
	E	Incorrect:	Product Status Account can be requested by the Project Manager at any time. This is likely to be required to support the Highlight Report. Ref 15.4.5.
5	A	Correct:	The stage budget should cover both the costs of products and the resources and management required to deliver them. Ref A16.1.
	B	Incorrect:	The budgets section of the Stage Plan covers time and cost, including provisions for risks and changes. Ref A16.2.
	C	Incorrect:	The budgets section of the Stage Plan covers time and cost, including provisions for risks and changes. Ref A16.2.
	D	Correct:	The budgets section of the Stage Plan covers time and cost, including provisions for risks and changes. Ref A16.2.
	E	Incorrect:	Time, cost and scope tolerances for the level of plan should be shown under a separate heading of 'Tolerances'. Ref A16.2.

Question: 7, Part: A, Type: CL			
1	A	Incorrect:	There is a positive tolerance of 1 week which can be allocated to any of the stages, as appropriate. Ref 10.3.1.2.
	B	Correct:	Tolerance is allocated based on the level of risk and confidence of estimates for any given stage. All project tolerance can be allocated to a single stage, but the risk of doing so must be assessed. Ref 10.3.1.2.
	C	Incorrect:	The project tolerance is approved by corporate/programme management. This cannot be affected by early completion of stages or Work Packages. Ref 10.3.1.1.
	D	Incorrect:	Additional unplanned resources may reduce timescales but this will require use of other tolerances, e.g. cost tolerances. Ref 15.4.8

2	A	Incorrect:	Tolerances stated in the Project Plan can be changed through formal change control and approval of corporate/programme management. Ref 10.3.4.
	B	Correct:	Tolerances stated in the Project Plan can be changed through formal change control and approval of corporate/programme management. Ref 10.3.4.
	C	Incorrect:	Where tolerance is forecast to be exceeded the exception procedure is followed and an Exception Plan created to replace the Project Plan. Ref 10.3.4.
	D	Incorrect:	Exception situations are dealt with as they occur and not left until the end of the stage. An exception assessment would be scheduled. Ref 10.3.4.
3	A	Correct:	A Product Description should be baselined when the plan containing the creation of that product is baselined. If the product is later changed, the Product Description must also pass through change control. Ref 7.3.3.3.
	B	Incorrect:	The project is not forecast to exceed tolerance. Ref 10.3.4.
	C	Incorrect:	Any change to a baselined product should first pass through change control. Ref 9.3.2.
	D	Incorrect:	Checkpoint Reports are created by the Team Manager, not the Project Manager. Ref 10.3.3.4.
4	A	Incorrect:	If a product has not been delivered to agreed timescales as a result of rework, the stage should not be delayed, the rework should be planned into the next stage. Ref 17.4.4.
	B	Incorrect:	There is no indication that the stage is forecast to exceed tolerance. Ref 10.3.4.
	C	Correct:	By checking the target sign-off date the Project Manager will know if there is an actual delay or whether the Marketing department has exceeded the time allocated for follow-up actions. Ref 17.4.4 / 10.3.3.2.
	D	Incorrect:	No products should be baselined until they are signed-off. Ref 9.3.2.
5	A	Incorrect:	There is no indication that a further project has been agreed and the production of a project mandate is not within the scope of the Calendar project.
	B	Incorrect:	This is not an expected benefit of this project and would not therefore appear in the Benefits Review Plan. Also, the Benefits Review Plan is updated at the end of each stage, not just the end of the project. Ref A1.
	C	Incorrect:	Exception Reports provide information to the Project Board when tolerance is forecast to be/or has been exceeded. Ref 10.3.4.
	D	Correct:	The Lessons Log captures lessons learned during the project that can usefully be applied to other projects. Notes should be made of any good and bad experiences in the use of the management and specialist products and tools as they occur. Ref 10.3.3.3.

6	A	Incorrect:	Checkpoint Reports are provided to the Project Manager, not the Executive. Also, an issue should be raised to the Project Manager if tolerance is forecast to be exceeded. Ref 10.3.3.4/10.3.4.
	B	Incorrect:	Team members do not have the authority to change a Stage Plan. If a product is late, the Project Manager may plan the remaining work into the next stage and amend the Work Package accordingly. Ref 10.3.3.1.
	C	Incorrect:	The Team Manager should raise this as an issue. If the Project Manager determines it is a project risk, the Project Manager should record it in the Risk Register. Ref 10.3.3.4.
	D	Correct:	All problems, questions and queries should be raised as an issue. Ref 10.3.4.

Question: 7, Part: B, Type: AR

1	False:	Management stages are determined primarily by the level of risk, major decision points and commitment of resources. The label design competition does not justify this level of control. Ref 10.3.2.1.	False:	The chosen label design is a deliverable within the project. Specialist products should be reviewed and approved as soon as they are completed, and not postponed until the end of the stage. Ref 16.4.2.
2	True:	It may be quicker to produce black and white photos, rather than full colour, thus reducing quality but saving time. Ref 15.4.8.	False:	The use of one tolerance to resolve the issues with another tolerance will depend on the objectives of the project. If quality is the focus then this will not be the first to go.
3	True:	Stage boundaries should be scheduled around key decision points for the Project Board. Ref 10.3.2.1.	True:	The production cost forecast provides a key decision point for the Project Board whether to continue with the project. This reason explains the assertion, therefore the answer is A. Ref 10.3.2.
4	False:	There is +1 week project tolerance, indicating the project can complete one week later than planned, NOT two, and still remain within tolerance.	False:	Negative project time tolerance does NOT indicate the latest permissible date, it indicates the earliest acceptable completion date, before exceeding tolerance. Ref 10.3.4.
5	False:	The Project Manager should first escalate exception situations to the Project Board. They may then need to escalate to corporate management. Ref 10.3.1.1.	True:	Project tolerance is set by corporate or programme management. Any forecast to exceed this must be escalated accordingly. Ref 10.3.1.1.

6	True:	The projected costs will influence the Project Board decision to proceed with stage 3. All Project Board decisions are made during the Directing a Project process. Ref 10.3.1.2.	False:	Products are reviewed and approved by nominated parties as and when they are completed. Not at the end of each stage. Ref 16.4.2.

Question: 8, Part: A, Type: MG		
1	Correct [B]:	The Plan is approved, this includes the PID for the photos. This requirement was not included within the original composition of the photos; it is therefore a request for change. Ref Table 9.1.
2	Correct [A]:	'May' tells us this has not yet happened, and is therefore a concern at this time. A problem or concern is any other issue (not an Off-specification or a RFC) that the Project Manager needs to resolve or escalate. Ref Table 9.1.
3	Correct [B]:	The list of customers has been approved. Once approved a product should not be changed without an authorized request for change. Ref Table 9.1.
4	Correct [A]:	There is not a problem with the schedule, this is not off-specification. There is an issue with the performance of a team member. This is a problem that needs to be addressed by the Project Manager. Ref Table 9.1.
5	Correct [C]:	The chosen label design is off-specification because the product does not contain the correct data, as specified. Ref Table 9.1.
6	Correct [A]:	The probability of this risk is 100%, it is now an Issue Report. This is neither a request for change nor an off-specification. It is therefore a problem. A problem or concern that the Project Manager needs to resolve or escalate. Ref Table 9.1.

Question: 8, Part: B, Type: MG		
1	Correct [B]:	Maintaining a record of all copies issued will provide a list of who has been issued products and which versions they have. Ref 9.3.2.
2	Correct [E]:	The recall of superseded versions from all copyholders would ensure that only the correct products are in circulation. Ref 9.3.2.
3	Correct [C]:	The Record of links between versions and the Issue Report that caused its change will provide an audit between each version of a product and a reference to further information regarding the change. Ref A5.2
4	Correct [F]:	The Retention of all master copies ensures that the original is protected, traceable and always available. Ref 9.3.2.

5	Correct [A]:	The Product Status Account tracks products through their design, development, review and approval, providing a summary of product status. Ref 9.3.1.3
6	Correct [G]:	Maintaining a record of the relationships between products ensures that no product is changed without being able to check for possible impacts on related products. Ref 9.3.1.2.

Question: 9, Part: A, Type: CL			
1	A	Incorrect:	This is a pre-defined plan (updated Managing a Stage Boundary) stating when and how the expected benefits of a project should be measured. It would not identify alternative ways in which products might be used. Ref A1.
	B	Incorrect:	This records events that went well or badly. It would not record alternative ways to benefit from the deliverable of a project. Ref A14.
	C	Incorrect:	The project is not forecast to exceed tolerance in terms of cost and time, we are not therefore in exception. Ref A10.
	D	Correct:	When closing a project prematurely any value created to date and any gaps left by the cancellation of the project are raised to corporate/programme management in the End Project Report as part of the follow-on actions recommendations. Ref A9.
2	A	Incorrect:	A number of actions specific to the project's products may be required after the project has closed. This is past tense, the event has happened. There is no action recommended. Ref A8.
	B	Correct:	Nothing can be done to resolve this now, but future projects may learn from this experience. A review of what went well, what went badly and any recommendations for corporate/programme management consideration are recorded in the Lessons Report. Ref A15.
	C	Incorrect:	Closure notification is simply a communication to all interested parties that the project is coming to a close. It would not communicate anything about the disruption caused. Ref 18.4.5.
	D	Incorrect:	This is not a risk, this is past tense and the event has happened.
3	A	Incorrect:	This is a plan of how and when benefits should be measured. It does not communicate the closure of the project to interested parties. Ref A1.
	B	Incorrect:	This report compares the objectives with the outcomes, the plan 'v' actual of the project. It does not communicate the closure of the project to interested parties. Ref A8.
	C	Incorrect:	A number of actions specific to the project's products may be required after the project has closed. Any outstanding invoices, etc, need to be received prior to project closure. This is not an activity post project closure. Ref A8.
	D	Correct:	The Project closure notification advises those who have provided the support infrastructure and resources for the project that these can now be withdrawn. This should indicate a closing date for costs being charged to the project. Ref Glossary.

4	A	Incorrect:	This is a plan of how and when benefits should be measured. The objectives or outcomes are stated in the PID and their achievement documented in the End Project Report. Ref A1.
	B	Correct:	An End Project Report is used during project closure to review how the project performed against the version of the PID used to authorize the project. A review of the project objectives is recorded in the End Project Report. Ref A8.
	C	Incorrect:	The project is not forecast to exceed tolerance in terms of cost and time, we are not therefore in exception. Ref A10.
	D	Incorrect:	The Project closure notification advises those who have provided the support infrastructure and resources for the project that these can now be withdrawn. This is simply a communication and does not assess what has been delivered. Ref Glossary.
5	A	Incorrect:	This is a plan of how and when benefits should be measured. The objectives or outcomes are stated in the PID and their achievement documented in the End Project Report together with any proposed actions. Ref A1.
	B	Incorrect:	The project is not forecast to exceed tolerance in terms of cost and time, we are not therefore in exception. Ref 10.
	C	Correct:	When closing a project prematurely any value created to date and any gaps left by the cancellation of the project are raised to corporate/programme management in the End Project Report as part of the follow-on action recommendations. Ref A8.
	D	Incorrect:	This is not a risk, it is stated as fact with 100% probability.
6	A	Incorrect:	The Issue Register will be archived with the project files, any outstanding issues being transferred to the follow-on action recommendations in the End Project Report. An assessment of what went well and what went badly is the Lessons Report. Ref A15.
	B	Incorrect:	A number of actions specific to the project's products may be required after the project has closed. This is stated as a learning opportunity, there are no actions suggested.
	C	Correct:	Future projects may learn from this experience. A review of what went well, what went badly and any recommendations for corporate/programme management consideration are recorded in the Lessons Report. Ref A15.
	D	Incorrect:	This is past tense. It has happened, it is therefore not a risk.

Question: 9, Part: B, Type: AR

1	False:	Countering the decline in orders is a positive consequence (benefit) of this project that cannot be measured until 12 months after the project has closed.	False:	The Benefits Review Plan is created in the Initiating A Project process. Ref 14.4.7. It is reviewed and may be updated at the end of each stage and during the Closing a Project process. Ref 18.4.3.

2	False:	The Acceptance Method in the Project Product Description will state the means by which the acceptance will be confirmed. This could simply be done by confirming all the products have been approved.	True:	The Project Product Description contains the Acceptance Criteria of the Project Product and the standards and processes that will need to be applied to achieve this. Ref A21.1 / 18.4.1.
3	False:	The Project Scenario explains that the prepared calendar pack must be ready by 30 November, but there is also a time tolerance of +1 week.	True:	This report is produced by the Project Manager toward the end of the project, during the Closing a Project process, and is used by the Project Board to evaluate the project and authorize closure. Ref A8.1.
4	True:	The final management stage of a PRINCE2 project should include the products of project closure. The Closing a Project process takes place within the final management stage. Ref 11.2.4.	True:	The Closing a Project process takes place towards the end of the final management stage. Closure is not a stage, it is a process. This is the reason for the assertion. The answer is A. Ref 18.3.
5	False:	Whilst handover of responsibility for the products is necessary during the Closing a Project process, this contract is not in the scope of this project. The product should be handed over to the Marketing department.	False:	Where a product requires a lot of potentially expensive support and maintenance, the Project Manager should ensure that a suitable service agreement or contract is in place. Ref 18.4.3.
6	False:	The Closing a Project process should be followed at the end of stage 3, rather than the Managing a Stage Boundary process, as this is the final stage. Ref 17.2.	True:	At the end of each stage the Project Manager should update the Project Initiation Documentation (e.g. the Business Case, Project Plan, project approach, strategies, project management team structure and role descriptions). Ref 17.2.

And finally... 5

5 And finally...

If you have managed to get this far you are as ready for the PRINCE2 examinations as you are ever likely to be. It remains only to wish you the little bit of luck that we all need to make a success of any venture. If you are still not confident of your knowledge of PRINCE2, or your ability to convince an examiner that you are able to apply it to a given situation, you should consider attending an APM Group accredited training event and, perhaps, try to gain more experience in using the method. Further details of accredited training organizations can be found at the APM Group's website www.apmgroup.co.uk/PRINCE2.

Good luck with your preparation.

August 2009

Further information

Further information

FROM THE OFFICE OF GOVERNMENT COMMERCE

PRINCE2 is part of a suite of guidance developed by the Office of Government Commerce (OGC), aimed at helping organizations and individuals manage their projects, programmes and services. Where appropriate, this guidance is supported by a qualification scheme and accredited training and consultancy services.

Management of Risk: Guidance for Practitioners

Projects exist in a fundamentally uncertain world and, as such, effective management of risk is crucial to managing the delivery of the project's products, their outcomes and the ultimate benefits that have been identified.

Management of Risk (M_o_R®) puts the management of project risk into the context of the wider business environment.

Managing Successful Programmes

Managing Successful Programmes (MSP™) represents proven programme management good practice in successfully delivering transformational change across a wide range of public- and private-sector organizations. It provides a framework to direct and oversee the implementation of a set of related projects and activities in order to deliver outcomes and benefits related to the organization's strategic objectives.

Portfolio Management Guide

The Portfolio Management Guide explains the key principles of portfolio management, from the experience of public- and private-sector organizations in the UK and internationally. It provides practical advice on setting up a portfolio management function, illustrated with real-life examples, and concludes with a section on further advice and guidance. The main audience for this guide are the teams responsible for coordinating programmes and projects, particularly those providing support for investment decisions and reporting on progress to the management board. A working knowledge of programme and project management and progress reporting is assumed.

Portfolio, Programme and Project Office

Portfolio, Programme and Project Office (P3O®) provides guidance on how to define, establish and operate a portfolio, programme or project office. It covers the range of functions and services that P3Os may provide and includes references to the techniques that may be employed.

Portfolio, Programme and Project Management Maturity Model

The Portfolio, Programme and Project Management Maturity Model (P3M3™) is a reference guide for structured best practice. It breaks down the broad disciplines of portfolio, programme and project management into a hierarchy of key process areas (KPAs).

The hierarchical approach enables organizations to assess their current capability and then plot a roadmap for improvement prioritized by those KPAs which will make the biggest impact on performance.

PRINCE2 Maturity Model

The PRINCE2 Maturity Model (P2MM™) describes a set of KPAs required for the effective implementation and use of PRINCE2 within an organization. This is P2MM's core value: while the PRINCE2 manual describes how to manage a single project, it does not include any processes on how to embed PRINCE2, whereas P2MM does.

P2MM describes key practices aligned with the PRINCE2 processes and components to enable repeatable application of the method (Level 2), and goes further to describe the key practices required to institutionalize the method (Level 3) as a standard business process for managing projects.

OGC Gateway Review Process

OGC Gateway Review is a well-established project and programme assurance review process, which is mandated for all UK government high-risk programmes and projects. OGC Gateway Review delivers a peer review, in which independent practitioners from outside of the individual programme/project use their experience and expertise to examine progress and assess the likelihood of successful delivery of the programme or project. It is used to provide a valuable additional perspective on the issues facing the internal team, and an external challenge to the robustness of plans and processes. This service is based on good practice, and there are many similar examples

across all business sectors of this type of peer review designed to provide assurance to the owner of the programme or project.

Full details of the OGC Gateway Review Process are available from the OGC website: www.ogc.gov.uk

Achieving Excellence in Construction

Achieving Excellence in Construction procurement guidance is contained within a set of eleven guides and two high-level guides. It builds on departments' recent experience, supports future strategy and aligns with the OGC Gateway Review process.

Through the Achieving Excellence in Construction initiative, central government departments and public-sector organizations commit to maximize, by continuous improvement, the efficiency, effectiveness and value for money of their procurement of new works, maintenance and refurbishment.

ITIL® Service Management Practices

ITIL is the most widely accepted approach to IT service management in the world. Providing a cohesive set of best-practice guidance drawn from the public and private sectors across the world, it has recently undergone a major and important refresh project.

IT Service Management (ITSM) derives enormous benefits from a best-practice approach. Because ITSM is driven both by technology and the huge range of organizational environments in which it operates, it is in a state of constant evolution. Best practice, based on expert advice and input from ITIL users, is both current and practical, combining the latest thinking with sound, common-sense guidance.

FROM TSO (COMPLEMENTARY PUBLICATIONS)

APMP for PRINCE2 Practitioners

This study guide enables candidates familiar with PRINCE2 to prepare for the APMP exam. It provides APMP exam candidates with a single source of reference material that covers all aspects of the APMP syllabus, including both pre-course and on-course material, whilst aligning it to the PRINCE2 method. This enables PRINCE2 practitioners (or project management staff working within a PRINCE2 environment) to expand their project management knowledge to cover all topics within the APMP syllabus.

APMP for PRINCE2 Practitioners (2008). The Stationery Office, London.

Focus on Skills series (set of three books)

The Focus on Skills series explores the various 'soft skills' that are demonstrated by effective project and programme managers, as the day-to-day coordination, motivation and communication aspects of project and programme management are very similar.

Leadership Skills for Project and Programme Managers (2008). The Stationery Office, London.

Team Management Skills for Project and Programme Managers (2008). The Stationery Office, London.

Communication Skills for Project and Programme Managers (2008). The Stationery Office, London.

Agile Project Management: Running PRINCE2 Projects with DSDM Atern

This ground-breaking publication shows how users can combine the strength of both approaches so that they complement each other and create a new, best-of-breed framework, suitable for all project environments. Based on PRINCE2 and DSDM Atern, the most established and internationally recognized project management approaches, this title explores the differences between the two approaches before showing where they overlap and how they can be integrated. While DSDM Atern is a project management methodology in its own right, this new publication sits within the PRINCE2 suite of titles.

Agile Project Management: Running PRINCE2 Projects with DSDM Atern (2007). The Stationery Office, London.

Improving Project Performance using PRINCE2 Maturity Model

PRINCE2 is cited as the most widely used project management method worldwide. But, while the PRINCE2 manual describes how to manage a single project, it does not include any guidance on how to embed PRINCE2 into an organization.

Such guidance is now available: this publication describes the organizational processes and practices required for the effective implementation of PRINCE2 as an organizational standard. It includes guidance on assigning ownership, tailoring the method, training, integrating PRINCE2 with other management systems and establishing quality assurance mechanisms to gain a continuous improvement capability.

In reading *Improving Project Performance using the PRINCE2 Maturity Model* you will discover how organizations can gain full value from the PRINCE2 method. It contains practical advice on using the OGC's PRINCE2 Maturity Model (P2MM) and shows how P2MM can be used.

Improving Project Performance using the PRINCE2 Maturity Model (2007). The Stationery Office, London.

ACCREDITED CONSULTANTS

The APM Group accredits a network of accredited consultancy organizations (ACOs) worldwide. Each ACO employs at least one APM Group registered consultant, accredited in one or more of the following specializations:

- Programme and project management consulting
- PRINCE2 consulting
- Managing Successful Programmes (MSP) consulting
- Management of Risk (M_o_R) consulting
- P3O consulting

Registered consultants can help organizations by providing support and expertise in process implementation, and they have exclusive rights to assess organizations against the Office of Government Commerce Portfolio, Programme and Project Management Maturity Model (P3M3) and the PRINCE2 Maturity Model. They can help organizations benchmark their programme, project and risk management processes, and provide the support required in order to drive further improvement.

Index

Index